ALWAYS ARGUE IN THE NUDE

...and other ridiculously helpful guidance for settling in to a happy marriage

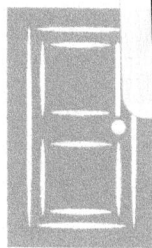

HILDA PAPER

Blue Poodle Press™

Cover Design: Jacob Hart
hart.jacob@gmail.com

Cover Photo: Rick Quevedo
@rcqcreative

ISBN 978-0692390917

Blue Poodle Press™
21781 Ventura Blvd   Suite 567
Woodland Hills, CA 91364
www.BluePoodlePress.com

With gratitude for those who helped us,

and

applause for those who are working to make their marriage "Heaven on Earth"

The gift goes on...

Hilda

A WORD ABOUT THE TITLE

Well of course it's not entirely serious. It's a quote from a dear friend who gives this advice to couples in a marriage-preparation class. The line always gets a laugh, of course. In fact, she and her husband keep the couples laughing throughout their presentation, which is pretty amazing, considering that they teach on sexual intimacy, and most of the couples arrive for class that day so nervous they're barely breathing.

As a piece of advice, "Always argue in the nude" is a little bit of silliness wrapped up in a whole lot of wisdom, to encourage couples to have fun and play together. In fact, that is the right attitude to take into every aspect of marriage. Marriage is a serious business in which two people learn to help each other lighten up!

The first years of a marriage present their own unique challenges, and this book was written to help you get through them and on the way toward your 50th anniversary.

You can't always argue in the nude—you would probably get thrown out of your favorite restaurant if you tried it—but you can have a marriage that is even more wonderful than you could have imagined.

Contents

Foreword

Have you ever wanted to sit down with a wise woman—mother, grandmother, aunt, or older friend—who really understands what you are going through in your marriage? Read this book. Have you longed for someone who can be with you through your pain, confusion and uncertainty? Read this book. Have you wished for someone who has overcome much and lived life successfully, enabling her to take your hand and guide you along the path? Please take a positive step and read this book.

Hilda writes about life and marriage with wisdom that does not come from academic studies, though they have their place, but from a life well-lived and from deep reflection on her marriage and children. She writes like she speaks, with humor and directness that are both refreshing and reassuring. At the same time, it is deeply personal and compelling. She will help you believe that you can successfully overcome whatever difficulty you may face in your marriage.

Lloyd Hamner
Licensed Marriage and Family Therapist
Director, California Christian Counseling Center
Van Nuys, California

Introduction:
READ THIS FIRST!

Why did you get married?

Maybe you imagined having someone there at the end of every day who would be on your side to love and encourage you, someone who would build you up after you've spent a tough day in the cold, cruel world.

But maybe it isn't working out that way. Home is not the peaceful, wonderful place you imagined. Home is a place of conflict and tension. These days it may be hard to come home. You're confused and upset about the rotten condition of your young marriage.

I know exactly how you feel because I lived through it. Let me assure you that there are answers, and you can create that safe haven you always wanted.

Not what I had in mind

Nobody gets married planning to get divorced, but a lot of people get married *fearing* that they will get divorced. It may sound weird, but *being afraid* of a divorce can actually *bring one on*.

There is nothing terribly complicated about making a good marriage. You just have to lay down your life for the person you love, and the person you marry has to lay down his or her life for you. If you are afraid of divorce, you've got to get that fear out in the open and face it down.

And you've got to *create* joy in your married life—not just wait for it to find you. Most important in sustaining a good marriage, you've got to learn to forgive each other, because no matter who you marry, I guarantee that your spouse is going to turn out to be a flawed human being who will need lots and lots of forgiveness.

And, oh, yes, so will you!

If you grew up in the church and had solid Christian teaching, you are probably familiar with these ideas. But the best Christian teaching is useless if you can't put it into practice in your life. So this little book had better contain truths that will work for anybody, Christian or not! Sure, I wish everyone knew the benefits of life in Christ, but that's a whole 'nother issue, so don't worry. I'm not going to grab you by the shoulders and try to talk you into anything. The only "preaching" you'll find here will be the constant encouragement of someone who lived through a hell of a marriage and then learned how to make it heaven on earth.

So let's talk about why *your* marriage isn't heaven on earth yet.

Baby, where did our love go?

If you are one of those couples who "did everything right," but it still doesn't seem to be working, you are probably pretty confused at this point. After all, you're both committed to living out your faith in marriage. You're members of a good church, and, most important, you are sure that you married the "right" person. When you got engaged, you read all the books, took a marriage preparation class, watched all the videos, and even did some pre-marital counseling. You got married feeling secure in the knowledge that you were in love and doing everything possible to build on a solid foundation.

And yet, none of that preparation seems to be helping now. That solid foundation seems to be crumbling beneath your feet. You feel lost, and what's worse, you're not even sure you *like* your spouse any more, let alone *love* him or her. With every day that goes by, you feel yourself retreating inside, pulling back not only from your spouse, but from everything you thought you knew and believed in.   You feel increasingly phony, maintaining the correct outward behavior, horribly aware that your inner feelings are bordering on panic.

Or maybe...

It could be that you waited a long, long time for the right one to come along, and then you found someone absolutely perfect, so you jumped right in to marriage. You never dreamed that you would have problems, because you had waited so patiently and you were so sure you had found the right person. And yet here you are, not only unhappy, but completely disenchanted.

Or...

Perhaps the two of you went together for years and years, and marriage seemed inevitable. Everyone around you seemed to confirm that the two of you were "meant to be," and you expected those comfortable, familiar feelings that you had enjoyed for so long to continue on into your marriage. But now everything you thought you knew about your spouse is up in the air, and he or she feels the same way. After all these years, the two of you don't feel as if you know each other anymore.

And then there's always the case...

If you two lived together before you got married, yours may be the most baffling situation of all. For a year, or two, or three, or more, you were happy, faithful, and comfortable. You considered yourselves married in every way except legally. Then you went ahead and tied the knot, and that's when everything fell apart. What's *that* about?

No matter what your specific story may be, at this point you feel exhausted, desperate, and angry. You've thought about it so much you're tired of thinking about it. And lately, more and more often, all you think about is getting out. You just can't figure out why it feels as if you've made the biggest mistake of your life, when it all looked so good a little while ago.

How could things have changed so fast?

How could it be so *bad*, when you *both want it to be good*?

Why isn't it working?

You may not have any idea what happened to create the condition you are in—all you know is that your life has become dreary and draining, and there is a growing sense of desperation about the future. You're irritable all the time, and it seems as if the harder you try, the angrier and more irritable you get. You try to maintain a good "front" for the world, but things are slipping, and you're having a harder and harder time holding things inside. You feel as if you're going to burst. Sometimes you think you're losing your mind, and maybe—and this is really frightening—you have started to take it out on your spouse. Conversations erupt in anger, seemingly out of nowhere. Your spouse may get angry right back at you, or may just withdraw. It's not good.

You may be completely stumped as to what went wrong, or you may think you know *exactly* what is going wrong. In either case, at this point there doesn't seem to be anything else to do but get a divorce. The relationship that seemed as if it would bring you lifelong joy has turned out to be a burden and a pain. Nothing prepared you for this. You feel isolated, as if you're the only person whose marriage ever turned sour this quickly. What on earth happened?

Has anyone else ever gone through this?

You might be surprised to learn that your situation is far from unique, and that the feelings you're having are so common, they could be called *normal*.

The sad statistic is that half of all divorces occur within the first seven years of marriage. You don't want to add to that number—you never thought you'd *ever* have to be seriously considering divorce—but the way things have been lately, you haven't been able to think of any other path.

Believe it or not, despite the fact that you may spend all day every day feeling that your relationship has turned to ashes, all is not lost. In fact, it is entirely possible that you are right on the brink of a breakthrough. You may feel exhausted and unprepared, but the truth is that you might be in the best possible condition to finally learn how to make your marriage work, so that you can have the lifelong happy marriage you want.

Welcome to "discovery time"!

The early years of marriage are an adventure in discovery. You learn things about each other. You also learn about yourself—things that may surprise you. (I never knew I had a terrible temper until I was married.) And of course you learn things about the nature of marriage that you can't possibly learn until you *are* married.

No matter how long you have known each other and how well you prepared for marriage, there are going to be big and small surprises in your first few years together, and some of those surprises may cause you disappointment.

But unhappy surprises do *not* have to lead you to divorce.

In fact, those surprises—or shocks—may actually help you to face things about *yourself* and *your* life that you might have been ignoring. We humans are awfully good at ignoring things, especially things that are scary or upsetting. We become experts at avoiding situations that make us uncomfortable, even if that means we cut ourselves off from something we really want.

So maybe you're not on the edge of a disaster. Maybe you're on the edge of a great breakthrough in your life. If you are discovering brand-new things about your life and your marriage, this could be the end of the beginning.

Go back and read that last sentence very carefully.

Marriage is the beginning of a new life for two people. And the reality of marriage never matches up with whatever we imagine it to be. You've made a beginning—maybe a good beginning, maybe a not-so-good beginning. It's time to move into the real heart of marriage, in which you open yourselves to having more love for, and appreciation of, your spouse than you have ever known before—more love than you ever thought possible.

There is an old story which is often used in motivational training seminars, about a man who quit mining just three feet from one of the richest gold mines ever discovered. If you have been married for a short time and I've been describing your current condition pretty accurately so far, it is quite likely that you are "just this side" of finding riches, too. Digging through the parts of life that are hard as rock and full of muck is not easy, but the rewards *are* golden. One of the greatest rewards is the discovery that you have more strength and endurance than you ever knew you had. Take it from someone who has been through it. It really is worth it.

Just keep breathing—and reading.

Chapter One
Is this the end?

The way she chews gum annoys you. Was she always this way? Why didn't you notice that before? The way he throws himself down on the sofa makes you want to scream. Was he always this way? Why didn't it bother you before?

Does it mean you're falling out of love? Probably not.

Is your marriage doomed? Probably not.

Or perhaps I should say, in answer to those two questions: it probably doesn't have to be.

Yes, there are a few legitimate reasons for ending a marriage. But we're not here to talk about marriages with major issues; we're going to discuss the kind of unhappiness that happens in a young marriage to caring, honest people who feel as if they've somehow lost their way.

If you're dealing with a major problem, such as abuse, drug or alcohol addiction, or adultery, there is still hope—there is always hope—but you are probably going to need skilled professional help. There are couples who overcome such problems and go on to have happy, healthy marriages.

The honeymoon is over

So here you are, married maybe just a few months or a few years, and you feel as if the joy and beauty of your relationship have gone out the window.

For a long time it all seemed to flow so naturally. You got along well. It was easy to give, and it was *fun* to give. In fact, it felt like the most natural thing in the world to give. But nothing flows along any more, and nothing about your life together seems to come naturally. Lately it seems that everything about your relationship is difficult and painful, and that floating-on-air sense that you once had, of gliding along on a smooth path of love and romance, is gone. You keep looking back longingly, wanting it to be the way it used to be.

Well here's the bad news: that gliding feeling is gone for a while.

Now here's the good news: you're ready for the next stage of married life, the part where you make your life together even better than it was at the beginning—much better, in fact, than you could have dreamed.

Maybe you don't like hearing that things won't come easily any more, and maybe you don't believe it, but let me explain what I mean by "the next stage." It most definitely does *not* mean that life is going to remain as uncomfortable and grim as it has become lately. But it *does* mean that you are facing a wonderful opportunity for growth! And if you rise to the challenges of this stage, you will enter in to the real joy of living with your spouse, because the real joy is not the love that brought you together. The real joy is yet to come.

From vision to reality

The romance you had in the beginning, and that wonderful sense of sharing deeply with another human being, gave you a vision for your life. As you move into the day-to-day routine of married life together, that vision becomes the basis, or foundation, that guides you toward the life you now begin building together.

Sometimes it may seem by comparison that the memories of your early days together are just there to taunt and tease you about "the mess you got into," but I assure you, those memories are there to guide and direct you. Life happens only in "forward gear." So now you need to choose to get with the program, to move forward by making the choice to live that vision, by growing toward it together. If you have been looking back wishing it could be "the way it was at the beginning," you've been wasting time. It won't be like that ever again, but *it can be so much better than that*, if you set yourself in the right direction.

You may wonder how I can say this with such assurance. That's easy: I lived it. Our first years together were a lot of fun. Everything was easy. I loved giving and he loved giving, and our life together was everything a person could ever wish for in a relationship. It seemed that all the love songs in the world had come true for us. No one knew how to love the way we knew how to love.

And then, at some point during our third year together, it all turned sour. Now, I am not a person who keeps quiet when things aren't right, so I faced it head-on. I was sure that we could find a way to "get back" to that easy first love we had been enjoying. We went to a few sessions of counseling. But our relationship just wasn't right, and nothing we did seemed to help. In fact, the harder we tried, the angrier and more exhausted we became. (Sound familiar?)

Our relationship had progressed into a stage that required greater commitment and deeper intimacy, but we didn't recognize that fact.

The essence of our problem was that we needed to grow up, but at that point there was no one in our lives who could explain that to us, let alone guide us into it. Both my parents and his parents had gone through horrible mid-life divorces right around the time we had met. In both cases there was a third party involved, and the adulterous entanglements had led to their divorces. They were all nice people, but they had no wisdom to offer about how to be happily married.

What about our friends? They were also a nice bunch of people, but they were as clueless as we were. In fact, 40 years later, there is only one other couple still married from that old crowd. Some of our old friends have been married three times since then.

What kept us together? We had a couple of advantages.

For one thing, having your parents divorce is an incredibly painful experience, and it strengthens your resolve if you decide that you are never, never, never going to put your own children through it. My husband and I both had that big advantage. It was kind of a weird basis for commitment, but it was better than nothing.

And when things were at their worst, none of our parents wanted to take us back and we were too broke to set up separate households!

Of course the biggest advantage we had was that we stumbled into a community of happily married couples who not only knew how to stay in love for life, but knew how to teach it to others. Yes, such groups really do exist. And even though we found ours without looking, you don't have to sit around and hope. You can go right out and find one for yourself, right now today.

What's the difference?

One of the first things we learned was the difference between romantic infatuation and real love.

Romantic infatuation is a lot of fun, but it doesn't last, any more than a sunrise lasts all day. Yet some people spend their whole lives chasing after it. When one infatuation ends, they suffer for a while, and then move on to the next thrill.

But such people are essentially just adolescent brats, no matter how old they are, compared to those who choose to become mature adult human beings who are capable of lifelong love. Because no matter what else you thought you were getting into when you got married, you were entering into what may be the best shot you'll ever have at growing up.   And in a culture that encourages us to remain adolescent forever, that's no small thing.

What do I mean by that? Just look at the ads on TV or in your favorite magazine. See all those happy young people living it up?   Whatever they're doing, it's making them so very happy, happy, happy.   They're slender and attractive, driving nice cars, eating great food, and buying all the hip clothing, shoes, and accessories they could ever want.   They've got beautiful houses full of cool furniture and electronic gadgets.   Their hair looks great, and their skin looks great, and their teeth look great. They're even happy when they're working out.   And because they work out, they all look like models.

Oh, wait a sec.

They *are* models.

Now, no one is more in favor of free enterprise than I. But when advertisers are trying to persuade us that their products or services will enhance our lives, it can leave us with the subtle, nagging thought that our current lives are *just not enough*.

Every day we are bombarded with thousands of advertising messages. It's an endless parade of beautiful young people looking as if life is great because of the soft drink they're consuming or the new shoes they just bought or — especially — the car they drive. As a result of this constant stream of messages, it's easy for us to start feeling an edgy sense of emptiness. As we watch all the deliriously happy people in those advertisements who seem to be having the time of their lives drinking and eating and playing (and, of course, *shopping*), it can start to seem that we are the only people around who aren't enjoying every single moment of every single day. Even if we don't "buy into" the message that our lives are not complete without the newest car or the whitest teeth, the overall effect can be an erosion of contentment, and a preoccupation with how our lives don't "measure up."

This mental state is characteristic of the stage of development known as adolescence. No one is more preoccupied with what the other guys have, with being "in," and how they "measure up" comparatively, than an adolescent.

I am *not* saying you can blame advertisers for the state you're in, but despite the incredible health and wealth and comfort that have been created by our free enterprise system, there is a down side: we are encouraged to remain forever obsessed with ourselves, our needs, and our wants. And this is *not* the way to a happy marriage.

So let's compare the adolescent personality with the adult.

An adolescent thinks only of what he or she gets out of a relationship. A grown-up considers what will make his or her spouse happy, and may actually get more joy from giving than from getting.

An adolescent remains committed—until the commitment *costs* something, and then he or she quits. A grown-up understands that working at a relationship is an investment, not a cost.

An adolescent puts feelings first, and acts on those feelings. When the feelings change, the relationship is disposed of. A grown-up shows love consistently in word and in deed, knowing that feelings will come and go like the clouds on a summer day.

An adolescent wants things to work out *now*. A grown-up knows that growth is painful and takes time, and is content to make progress one small step at a time.

There it is. It's simple, but not easy. Difficult but not impossible. You may be asking, "Is it rewarding?" Oh, yes. It is rewarding in ways you cannot imagine. Oh yes, take it from me, indeed it is.

Forward, march!

The first thing you absolutely must do is to stop looking in the rear view mirror at "the way it used to be." It may seem as if you fell for an *illusion*, but what you had back then was a *vision*. And after you have a vision, there comes its implementation—making it real by living toward it, and that takes—yes, you've got it—time. You don't *feel* what you felt back then, but if you keep moving forward, you will have a relationship that is even richer and more solid—and more golden— than what first brought you together, because that's the way it works.

Do you ever think about building your "dream house"—one that you design and build yourself, putting it together piece by piece, just the way you want it? Well, now you have the opportunity to build your "dream marriage"—one that you design and build together piece by piece, just the way you want it.

We live in a culture that puts feelings first, and the hurting people and broken relationships all around us testify to the ridiculousness of the idea that we should trust and act upon whatever we feel. Are feelings important? Of course they are. But they are not all-important. They are not of primary importance. Feelings, by themselves, are nothing to build a life upon. Feelings *follow*; they should never be allowed to lead. Respect yourself, and the choice that you made. You are much too complex a creature to allow yourself to make decisions based on an aspect of your life that can change depending on what you ate for dinner!

Living the vision

The romantic spark that brought you together is supposed to kindle a long-lasting, dependable, enduring warmth that you continually "stoke" during a lifetime of devoted caring—caring that is exhibited in words and deeds.

When you've reached the stage of relationship beyond infatuation—when love, or perhaps we should say "loving," must be a conscious choice, when it doesn't just "come naturally" any more, and you have to make an effort—you're ready to grow up and learn what it is to love with your whole being—body, mind, soul, and spirit. It's a new beginning. From that point on, you take a big risk: you give with no expectation of return. From here on, you start thinking about your spouse's needs, training yourself to pay attention to what will make his/her life more joyful and fulfilling. Most important, you start a lifetime of *expressing gratitude for all he/she does for you.*

You're thinking, "Gee, that sounds like I've signed my life away." And, in case you didn't notice, that's exactly what you did, back at the marriage altar.

But here's the thing: at the same time you are giving everything of yourself to the person you married, that person is now going to be giving to you, with no expectation of return, thinking about meeting your needs, making a conscious effort to pay attention to whatever will make your life more joyful and fulfilling, and expressing gratitude for all you do for him or her. Your spouse is doing that because he or she also signed away the right to be selfish, back there at the marriage altar.

"Hey now," you're thinking. "This just might work out." And it will. Once you both start loving on a conscious level that way, you will both discover the secret of real, lasting, enduring-unto-wrinkles-and-gray-hair love.

What made you think you could do this, anyway?

Here's a question: what made you think you knew everything there was to know about how to sustain a happy marriage?

I'm not trying to be sarcastic.

People who want to be beauticians in the state of California have to go to school 40 hours a week for one full year, and then take an all-day examination before they can become licensed to give you a haircut.

Even becoming a licensed manicurist in the state of California requires 300 hours of training.

People who want to have a license to drive a car have to take lessons. They have to study their state's driving manual to learn the laws, and then they take a written and a behind-the-wheel test.

But people who want to get married don't need any training or preparation, and they aren't required to show any proof of competence whatsoever.

To obtain a marriage license in California, a couple must be unmarried and present themselves in person with a valid photo ID at a county clerk's office. Blood tests are not required. Proof of divorce may be required if the bride or groom had been previously married.

And that's it.

The person who cuts your hair had to put in a year of study and pass a test, but you were allowed to sign your life away by virtue of the possession of a photo ID card.

So please, if you aren't excellent at marriage—if you haven't made your home into heaven-on-earth yet—cut yourself some slack, please, just a little bit.

Mastery

Think of something you do really well. Perhaps you are a great cook, or you can diagnose and repair any car trouble in the world, or you can play the piano. Did you always do it as well as you can do it now? Of course not. You started out clunky, and you got better at it with time and effort. It will be the same with your marriage, as long as the two of you are willing to keep working at it.

Here's another thing about marriage: you didn't really know what you were getting into. Even if you studied marriage as hard as your hairdresser studied hair—full time for a year, that is—most of us don't fully understand a new venture until we're in the middle of it, hands-on, up-to-the-eyeballs. That's why beauty schools offer such cheap haircuts, you know. Yours could be the first real head of hair someone ever lays scissors on, and that cheap haircut could make you look like you'd walked through a ceiling fan, but someday that same person will be charging a fortune for his work and turning out beautifully styled cuts. With practice, practice, and more practice, a person's abilities improve.

There is no getting around it: living together in a marriage requires effort, and the quality of your effort is related to your attitude.

Some societies don't even bother allowing people to go through all the trouble of finding their own spouses. Many cultures have functioned on the basis of arranged marriage: parents and other elders simply inform a young person as to who his or her marriage partner will be. Then these two people, who have no choice, face marriage as a true partnership, a mutual enterprise for the purpose of maintaining the stability of the home, the family, and the larger culture. Happiness may or may not enter into it. This may sound barbaric to those of us who believe in romance and self-determination, and for sure it is a form of slavery in cultures in which women have no rights, but it certainly eliminates a frivolous approach. If there is equality between the man and woman, and both sets of parents choose someone kind and hard-working, a couple enters marriage in a sober frame of mind — as a partnership for the purpose of living a good life.

Plenty of couples do worse on their own.

Fear of failure

But here you are, having made your own selection, and now you're experiencing severe second thoughts.

How much is the *fear of divorce* a part of your life?

Let's talk about fear. Specifically, I caution you not to scare yourselves into divorce. What I mean by that is that, today, divorce is "in the air." I can't imagine any young couple starting out these days without at least a little fear, somewhere in the back of their minds, that "there will come a time…."

It wasn't always like this. Let me tell you how rare divorce was when I was a child in the 1950s: I knew exactly one person in my entire grade school whose parents were divorced. Her name was Mary, and she lived alone with her mother. Back then it was shocking to imagine someone growing up without a father in the home. It was horrible to think of, outrageous and weird. It was obvious to everyone that there was something deeply wrong about it, and Mary and her mother were regarded with a mixture of pity and wariness.

Now fast-forward to my son's fifth grade class, in 1991. He came home one day and announced that he was one of *only three kids* at his lunch table who still lived with their own father and mother.

And that's what I mean about divorce being "in the air" these days.

So it is entirely understandable that a newly married couple should have a sense that they are embarking on something rather dangerous, something that not many people succeed at.

Statistics do lie

But here's something else about those divorce statistics: we're all accustomed to hearing that "fifty percent of all marriages end in divorce." But that statistic is deceptive. Although divorce is more common than it used to be, you don't have to worry that you only have a fifty-percent chance of "making it." It's not the case that half of all the population gets divorced. There are still a lot of people who get married and stay married 'til death do them part. But there is also a large population of people who get married and get divorced, and re-marry and get divorced again, and then go for three, and even four. And those are the people who make the statistics look the way they do.

For example, Bob married Laurie and they have been married for over 30 years. His brother Bill married Jane and got divorced, and then married Sally and got divorced, and then married Alice. So between the two brothers there have been four marriages and two divorces. How do we describe the divorce statistics in that little "population"? There were four marriages, and two of them ended in divorce, so that means that half of all their marriages ended in divorce, right? Right, but all the divorces were by one brother. And that is exactly what is happening in the population at large. One group of people marry and divorce repeatedly, while the other group gets married and stays married. See what I mean about statistics being deceptive?

You don't have to live in fear, but you do have to acknowledge that you are afraid—so that you can overcome the fear. Hidden fear has the power to control your thoughts and actions. Acknowledged fear loses its strength. It's like the monster in the closet. Open the door.

I'm not saying you should deny the possibility. It is always important to look at the world around you and describe it accurately. Yes, divorce is everywhere, and a lot of nice, bright people end up going through it—people every bit as nice and bright as you and I.

So what makes the difference?

The most important thing you can do is stop looking for things to be cheap and easy. Nothing worthwhile in life is cheap and easy. Accept the fact that your first love was a vision and a promise, and decide that you will now do the real living-out of that vision.

Accept the fact that marriage holds the promise and possibility of making you a better person than you would otherwise have become, and that it will take work to make that happen! Look fear-of-divorce in its ugly face and say, "You're outta here."

There.

That feels better already, doesn't it?

Chapter Two
We did/didn't live together

There are a lot of ideas that seem very sensible but don't work at all when they're applied in real life.

In fact, entire governments have been based on totally ridiculous, unworkable ideas. Take socialism, for example, which is the idea that if a bunch of people take everything they own and put it all together and share it equally, then everybody will have what he or she needs. Sounds wonderful, doesn't it? But what happens when your fellow socialists turn out to be lazy bums who are willing to sit around while *you* work *twice* as hard, supporting them? Then it's not so wonderful.

One big problem with new ideas is that, when they are put into practice, there are always unintended consequences—results that were not expected and planned-for. Life is full of these types of surprises.

Over the past 40 years or so, living together without getting married has seemed to make a lot of sense for couples, and many of these couples move in together as a sort of rehearsal for marriage, thinking by doing so that they can "try before they buy."

But living together "to see if it works out" turns out to be just another one of those goofy ideas that seem on the surface to make sense and then turn out to have unintended consequences. That is, living together actually *creates* a set of problems that a couple would not otherwise have to deal with.

Still, it has become such a cultural commonplace that a lot of people think it is a sensible idea, and so people continue the practice, blindly falling off the same cliff as the folks who went ahead of them.

Psychologists and other professionals who study such things keep trying to come up with a good explanation for why it is that couples who live together before marriage are more likely to end up getting divorced than those who do not live together. After all, people have called the practice "trial marriage."

One theory is that the kind of people who prefer to live together are excessively afraid of failure, and that fear makes them panic easily. And so, when the normal ups and downs of a marriage-like relationship occur, people who have been mentally "hunkered down," just waiting for signs that "the relationship won't work out," are going to see signs of doom where more mature couples see the natural give-and-take that is necessary when learning to live with another person.

Another theory is that people who live together have "self-selected" as the kind of people who do not see value in commitment. They seek nothing beyond what is gratifying for them in the here-and-now. These individuals see "self" and "now" as all-important, and do not put any value on working through tough issues. They see relationships as disposable for a number of reasons, all related to their idea of fulfilling their own immediate needs, first and foremost. And so, their lives become a series of self-induced upheavals as they seek direct satisfaction from one relationship after another.

And of course, there are those who want only the fun of romantic infatuation, and when that ends, as it always does, they give up and move on.

We got married and that was the end of our relationship

We all know couples who lived together for years, got married, and soon afterward got divorced.

What probably happened was that these couples carried a distorted picture of marriage. While they were living together they thought of themselves as "free to leave any time." They had never seen marriage as anything more than imprisonment, so once they did take the step, they felt locked up. Their limited understanding of marriage led each of them to be in a low-level panic state from that point on, constantly looking for "escape," and of course, people who are in a panic and looking for escape are not exactly candidates for a joyful lifelong union. As far as they were concerned, they had been enjoying all the benefits of marriage without entering into a binding legal arrangement. Marriage added nothing to their lives except oppression—a sense that the walls were closing in on them.

If all you have ever looked at in getting married is the "down-side," then the unacknowledged fear of commitment may actually destroy your ability to have a happy marriage. If a person has always been afraid that getting married will make him or her feel trapped, and that person gets married anyway, three guesses as to what he or she is going to feel.

As we discussed in the first chapter, an unacknowledged fear can be the determining factor in any endeavor. When you're afraid of something and don't face the fear, you tend to focus on it obsessively, and give it more power in your life than it should have. I call it the "monster in the closet." When you're afraid of something and you avoid facing it, it just gets bigger and bigger in your imagination.

Living together is a very understandable, very human way of trying to deal with the very understandable, very human fear of relationship failure, but wisdom requires that we examine whether that choice leads to success or failure. Most couples who live together do not stay together. If you lived together, got married, and now your relationship stinks, you have a lot of company.

I speak from experience. In the space of three years I lived through my parents' divorce, the end of my first marriage, and then my in-laws' divorce. The best way to avoid divorce, as far as I could see, was not to get married in the first place!

When I met the man who has been my husband for the past several decades, we first lived together for five years. We thought we were intelligent enough to create the relationship we wanted and needed. It was only when our first child came along that we saw that there was something bigger than our own wants and needs. Our son's birth finally opened our eyes to the world beyond "me" and "now." We started to grow up.

But we didn't live together, and our marriage is a mess anyway

Marriage is *difficult*. Learning to live with another human being in love and trust and peace takes time. Yes, you avoided a whole boat-load of problems by not living together, but that doesn't mean you won't have to face challenges. Go find me a happily married couple who will tell you that they did everything right at the beginning and so they had no problems at all. Go ahead. Find them.

Yes, I'm scared

If you're reading this book together, it should be relatively easy for the two of you to take a deep breath, step back from the edge of the cliff, and acknowledge to each other that your fear of failure is huge.

There. That's step one, and it's a biggie. In fact, it's *the* biggie, and once you're past the fear of saying it out loud, you're halfway home, because what you've really said out loud is that your spouse is precious to you, and you don't want to lose your marriage.

The intense pressure that you have felt inside is released to an enormous degree by that one simple confession.

My spouse won't read the book

Couples working on their marriage often read books like this together. What if your spouse is hesitant to read this book with you?

Then when you say you are scared of failure, you are probably going to get one of two responses. The best response, of course, is that your spouse makes a similar confession, which will open up wonderful possibilities for your future.

"Jane, I'm so afraid that our marriage is not going to work out. Whenever we disagree, I start to imagine that you are tired of being with me and you're thinking of leaving. And so I start to think about leaving, but I realize that's crazy."

"Oh, John, I know what you mean. I start to feel tension between us, and I think that this isn't going to work out, and so I start to wonder if you're thinking about leaving."

A conversation like that can start to break the ice:

"Well I am *not* thinking about leaving. I am committed to you and to our marriage, and I'll do my part in making this work."

In fact, a conversation like that can give both of you a lot of reassurance. It can be the beginning of a deepening of the relationship, a search for solid ground to build life upon.

If you say, "I have been so afraid that we are going to break up," and in response your spouse says, "I know. I've been feeling that way, too. And I don't want to. I want this marriage to work." Wow, folks, you have just drawn closer to one another. You've each just reassured the other that you are tracking with each other as far as the climate in your home. You feel the tension and you want to release the tension and move forward. You've both acknowledged that you each regard your marriage as something important. That one conversation can release a lot of pressure. It's the basis for a new beginning, the way a gardener walks in and turns the earth to soften things up for a new planting. Maybe your spouse will even want to start reading this book!

And what if you confess your fear but your spouse doesn't share the same feeling? He or she can still be reassuring. Your spouse might even say something like, "Really? I know we haven't been as close lately. I didn't quite know how to describe what I've been feeling, so I didn't talk about it, but I didn't think it was that serious. Don't worry: I'm not thinking about leaving you." You opened the door to talk about mutual needs, and what it means to "feel close." In other words, you've put your feet on the path to growth, and you're moving in the direction of the real fulfillments of marriage.

The shut-down

Ah, but what do you do if you say, "I have been so afraid that we are going to break up," and in response you get:

"That's a stupid thing to say."

Or: "What's your problem?"

Or: "You've got no reason to feel that way"

—or any one of about a hundred other ways your spouse can push you away? Naturally, alarm bells will be going off in your head. But don't panic. What seems like total rejection may just be the reaction of a man or woman who is *even more scared of rejection* than you are Don't bounce off that initial hurt. Calm down. Somebody is going to have to be the grown-up in this situation, and it might as well be you.

Here's the easiest thing in the world for me to say, and one of the hardest things—at least it always is hard for me; maybe it's not hard for you—to realize:

Don't take it personally.

Yeah, right.

Your spouse is looking directly at you. In fact, it is one of the most intensely personal-feeling moments you have ever known. There are only the two of you in the room. You're in a cold sweat from all the emotions, and here I come saying "Don't take it personally." Sure.

But just remember: you are reading this book, and because of what you have read, you have gone through a thought process and come to a realization and taken a risk, while your spouse, who is not (yet) reading this book, just got hit with the thing that he or she is probably most scared of. That's why he or she wouldn't even read the book. And the rejection you got from him or her is a basic human psychological response whenever we feel attacked: we either hit back or try to hide. Psychologists call it the "fight or flight" mechanism. It's buried deep inside our brains, part of our basic survival response.

You will have to make a special effort to take that negative and turn it to a positive. You can start by realizing that your spouse is just a sweet, scared human being who wants love and is scared about maybe losing that love.

I'm the queen of taking-things-personally, so I completely understand if you would really like to say something awful, or just throw up your hands and walk out the door. But somebody's got to take the first steps toward maturity, and it looks as if you've just been elected.

Congratulations.
Now what?
Keep reading.

Chapter Three
We did everything right.
(So why does it all feel so wrong?)

Some people prepare carefully for marriage. They don't get married with fingers crossed, hoping it will work. They have always taken marriage seriously, and grew up understanding that it was an important step, perhaps the most important choice a person makes in life. They married a quality person, someone of good character, someone who held marriage in high regard, just as they did.

Maybe they knew each other for a long time as friends and a romantic relationship grew slowly. Or maybe they met and dated for a long time, both of them knowing in their hearts that they had found "the one," but not rushing into anything. They enjoyed their courtship, and then, when they became engaged, prepared for marriage very carefully, taking classes, reading books, watching videos, and filling in the workbooks. They talked and talked and *talked* with each other, and invested time together with good counselors.

They both felt strong and confident and ready. They made sure they had their finances in order, planned out when they would buy a house, and how often they would trade in their cars. They agreed on when they would start a family, and how many children they would have.

And here they are, in a life that feels as if all the air has gone out of it. Oh, there is nothing they can identify that is seriously wrong. But there is nothing really right, either.

Am I talking to you? My husband and I didn't do anything right, so I can't say what it must feel like, but I would imagine that there could be a real sense of frustration when a person who is accustomed to planning life carefully, who knows in his or her heart of hearts that this marriage is right, finds out that Something. Is. Just. Missing.

Let me say first that you have done wisely and well in establishing a solid foundation for your life. But no matter how well you prepare, nobody gets a free pass when it comes to the process of learning to live together in marriage. There is no substitute for experience, and there is no way to get experience without, um, getting experience. Remember what you are asking your husband or wife to do: live closely on a daily basis for the rest of his or her life with a highly imperfect human being: you! That's asking a lot of someone.

Yes, you did everything possible to prepare on an *intellectual* level—that is, you've got the head knowledge—but the challenges of marriage involve your whole being, and the habits of a lifetime. Marriage involves discoveries—not just about the person you are married to, but about yourself—that you never knew existed quite this way.

What to do?

Do you feel some isolation and embarrassment about the imperfect state of your union? Well, you can let yourself off your own hook. You're just a normal flawed human being married to another normal, flawed human being.

It will help a lot if you have a "young marrieds" group you can meet with on a regular basis. When you meet with other couples you'll find out that everyone is dealing with the adjustments and surprises of marriage. A local church might have such a group. And of course it always helps to have long-term, happily married people in your life whom you can confide in, *but not your parents!*

If you're re-married and closer to middle-age, you probably won't be comfortable with a group of twenty-somethings, and if you are facing the challenges of step-families, you won't have much in common with them, anyway. But you are not the only couple going through this particular set of circumstances. You can find people who are, or have gone through, the same adjustments at the same stage of life.

Stop trying so hard

If you were thinking that you were supposed to know how to do this, get over it. Marriage is an art, not a science. You'll get better at it, just by putting in the time and paying attention. You can't hurry the process, much as you'd like to. I just planted some tomatoes. I wish they were ready for tonight's dinner, but I'll have to wait about three months. Same thing with your marriage. Do the things you know are right, and let it grow.

And I can't say this too often: We're living in a time when marriage is disposable, and so everyone who gets married in this era enters into a general culture that says marriage is a matter of instant perfection or nothing. You are infected by that attitude. You almost can't help it, unless you were raised in a cave somewhere.

As a result of absorbing that attitude, people who get married these days can suffer performance anxiety unknown to previous generations. Everything that falls short of perfection is considered grounds for divorce. Uh-oh, is she bored? Oh dear, is he unhappy? Could the person you are married to be making a private decision to quit?

It takes time to develop trust, and this is true for everyone, no matter who you are or how deeply committed you are to your spouse. And while you are giving that time for trust to develop, the world around you is tearing at you, at your mind, bombarding you with the message that you should be having fun, *now*, and you deserve it, *now*, so why are you spending this time suffering?

As time goes on, there may be other revelations—not just about your spouse, but about yourself. You may discover that you have tremendous fears—of rejection, of abandonment, of being alone. You may discover that you do not consider yourself very lovable in the first place, and as a result you've started wondering who in the world would want you, and why they should.

You may find that you are more cynical, more sour, more negative and pessimistic than you realized. You may feel more anger at your spouse than you ever knew you were capable of feeling.

I guarantee that in ways large and small you will be surprised at the feelings that you experience as you enter more deeply into this relationship called marriage. There is no other relationship that offers you the *opportunity* to be sifted and purified, to grow and become a better person. These discoveries are not a side show; they are the main event. You are there together in order to create something more wonderful than you could have created on your own, to become someone more wonderful than you could have become on your own, and that is going to require patience and effort. You are in this broken-down old world, and you have been shaped by it without your awareness or consent. It just happens, and you must become conscious of the distortions, and then make a conscious decision to turn away from them. The best possible "you" is the one who spends life loving, giving, and trusting. But you knew that.

Chapter Four
Who ya gonna call?

It was not very long ago that you were sure the road ahead was paved with rose petals. You were looking forward to spending the rest of your life with the most wonderful person you had ever known. Looking back, you think that maybe you ignored a couple of little "red warning flags," but you're not quite sure. All you know is that right now you feel as if you are suffocating, locked into a house or apartment with someone you barely even *like* any more.

And it's embarrassing even to think about discussing this with anyone.

Maybe you go over and over a mental "list" of people you might confide in, and you can't come up with anyone.

You think about friends and family, and imagine that they would be shocked to learn that you two aren't blissful newlyweds. Remember all those happy faces at your wedding? How could you tell any of those people that things don't seem to be working out?

You think of all your single friends who envy you because you "found someone." You think of all your married friends who don't seem to have any problems.

And maybe you even think of all the people who would *love* to know that you are unhappy. You're sure you'll *never* tell any of them the truth.

You start to feel isolated, as if you are living on a desert island, and you start to feel like a big phony, keeping up an image with the outside world.

There has got to be someone you can talk to!

The worst

There is someone you absolutely must not confide in—and it may be the first person you think of: dear old Mom.

Does that surprise you?

There are a couple of reasons it is a terrible idea for either of you to go to your parents.

The first reason is that you need someone to give you an objective, detached view of your situation. Your mother and father protected you from the big, bad world for a couple of decades. You can't ask them to turn off all that care and concern now. The sense of protectiveness a parent feels toward a child is intense—often beyond rationality. I am a mom, and I hope I would have the strength not to get involved if either of my sons ever came to me wanting to discuss an unhappy marital situation, because if I listened to their problems I don't think I could respond in a way that was fair and helpful. Before they got married, I always figured I would respond with that old, instinctive, mother-tiger protectiveness: "You hurt my kid? I remove your face." However, now that I have the two most wonderful daughters-in-law in the world, my sons know they had better be good husbands or their Mama is going to give them what-for!

In any case, I could never be the calm and impartial third party a couple needs when they hit rough marital weather.

Although it may be tempting to go home and spill your guts, especially if you have had a close relationship with your Mom and/or Dad, resist that urge!

Mommies like to be mommies

Of course, you have to admit that part of the reason it is tempting to go home and talk with the folks *is* that they'd probably take your side, tell you that you don't have to put up with that mean old husband, or that selfish wife, make you some hot cocoa, and tuck you in with your teddy bear!

Please, please be careful where you seek comfort.

Remember what I said earlier about marriage being your best shot at growing up? This is one of those occasions when you have got to stand apart from your parents. You moved away from home, physically speaking. Now you've got to "move away" in a different sense, as you create intimacy with your spouse, and put a little distance between yourselves and all of your parents.

When you got married, you and your spouse formed a private circle that includes only the two of you (and whatever children you have). *Neither set of parents belongs in the middle of your marriage circle.* In fact, it is very likely that there may be times when you must protect yourselves from their involvement. You want to grow forward, not slip backward, as you deal with the challenges in your marriage.

The other big reason

Besides all that, there is another important reason you never, never, never want to "bad-mouth" your spouse to your family, and that reason is that talking with your parents when you and your spouse are at a low point will create problems for you down the road.

When two people marry, they bring, essentially, a total stranger to their respective families of origin, and, by marrying that person, make that stranger a part of the family. This process of acceptance takes time, just as it took time for the two of you to think of yourselves as a couple. It is important to respect the fact that, just as it took you time to get to know each other, it takes time for your families to get to know their new family member. Most people would agree in theory that marriages will have their ups and downs, but when the actual "downs" come along, people tend to lose their perspective. The old saying that "blood is thicker than water" refers to that phenomenon. It isn't always the case, but you can usually rely on blood family to take the part of the one they grew up with. And they won't ever forget that someone hurt "one of their own."

When you come through a tough time with your spouse, you don't want any "hangover" of bad feelings between your beloved and your parents. So zip it! Your parents and other relatives may see things going on between the two of you, and they may ask, but if you are wise, you'll shut them down with a mild but firm request that they respect the fact that you have to work things out on your own.

Oops

OK, so you're reading this, and you've already gone to your parents. It's not too late. Tell them you made a *big* mistake by confiding in them, and say that you hope they'll understand that you are going to work out your problems with your spouse. Tell them that you would appreciate it if they would try to keep a balanced outlook, and that you hope they will try to understand that you should not have said anything which might prejudice them against their son- or daughter-in-law. It's a little like trying to put the toothpaste back in the tube, of course, but it will help. You may have to repeat this a few times if they make comments in the future, but at least you've laid the groundwork for maintaining your marital privacy.

Another really bad idea

There is another temptation that should be resisted just as strongly at those times when you feel as if you're going to burst if you don't talk to someone.

It is just a fact of human nature that we often try to avoid facing the things that overwhelm and frighten us. One way to avoid difficult situations is to wallow in misery with people who remain stuck in the same kind of failure. Cynical friends who are bitter after disastrous divorces or who have had a series of unhappy relationships can give you a cheap form of comfort, but their negativity can limit your horizon to the point that you, too, can see only the "down-side" to your situation.

Friends who have given up on their marriages are likely to confirm your worst fears about what is going on in your own marriage. "Misery loves company" was never more true than in this instance. If you seek the kind of "reassurance" you can get from people who believe that a happy marriage is just a matter of good luck—because they themselves do not or did not have success in marriage—you are selling yourself and your marriage short. If you have been spending time with people who are bitter or unhappy, it's probably time to take a closer look at your "support system." No matter how close you have been with these friends, face the fact that bitter, cynical, unhappy people are not going to lead you in the right direction, although they may offer a perverse kind of temporary break from the gloom.

This is a crucial time in your life, and it is important that you look not only at your marriage but at the people you turn to for help and advice. You are in the middle of grow-or-die time, and the people in whom you confide will make all the difference in your world and the way you spend the next 60 years of your life.

The other shoe drops

There is another lousy thing that can happen when you're in the middle of a difficult situation. We've all had the unhappy experience of confiding in the wrong person, and finding out that that person, for whatever reason, utterly rejects you for it.

There was a time in my life when everything seemed to be going to pieces, and I went to visit my two best friends, Pam and her husband Bob, to talk about it. When Bob opened the front door of their house, I burst into tears. Instead of expressing concern, he gave me a quizzical look and kept his arm stiffly stretched in front of him, with his hand on my shoulder, literally keeping me at arm's length as if I had a contagious disease. He let me into the house and pushed me toward Pam, who stood across the room with her arms folded across her chest and said coldly, "I have no sympathy for whatever it is you're going through. You have a lot of talent and you should make more of your life than you have." Then she offered me a cup of tea! I stumbled out of their house and ran to my car and drove away.

I found out just a few days later that I was in the early weeks of my first pregnancy, so hormone imbalance probably accounted for my distress and emotionalism. When Bob and Pam found out, they congratulated me, completely ignoring their own rejecting actions! But I had learned a terrible lesson about how much I could not trust them, and our friendship never was the same.

When you go to people who cannot "handle" your emotions or your confusion, that doesn't signify anything about *you* being deficient. On the contrary, it tells you everything about *their* deficiency in being unable to respond to you in a time of need. And, while you do have to acknowledge how much it hurts to be rejected, and how much it hurts to find out that you've been spending time with people who really don't accept the "whole you," you do have to forgive them their own immaturity and inability to help.

That doesn't mean you have to go on with them as before, because you pretty much can't ever do that, but it doesn't mean you end the relationship on the spot, either. It's just awfully, awfully painful to go through when you're already feeling that your life is falling apart.

But that's the way growth happens. And sometimes we grow out of old relationships when we are moving toward greater maturity. I guess maybe it shouldn't be such a surprise that, when you hit a rough patch in your marriage, you are going to learn about the character and integrity of a few other people in your life, as well! Sometimes we would rather not face some of the things we find out about people we thought we could rely on, because there is a terrible sense of loss when we find that a friendship is not as solid as we had always thought.

Marriage is the only relationship on earth in which two people stand before witnesses and vow to protect and nurture their connection. Everyone else in your life (except your children) stands outside that circle, and anyone who would say or do anything to detract from that central relationship should be kept far, far away.

Admit your ignorance and look for help

It may be difficult to admit that a big, grown-up person like yourself, a person who knows how to do a lot of things very well, doesn't know how to have a happy marriage.

But why did you expect that you would automatically know how to have a happy marriage? Even if you *had* read all the books, and even if your parents *are* the two most happily married people on the face of the earth, everybody gets to have his or her own custom-made, mind-boggling frustrations and conflicts—situations that you and your spouse must work out together. You wouldn't want to live someone else's life, would you?

Maybe the reason we get ourselves in so much trouble is our wonderful "can-do" American spirit. We jump right into a situation with an optimistic outlook, believing that we can do anything we set our minds to. We get married believing that we'll figure out how to be happily married—that we can simply make it come true as an act of our will. And in a sense, that's true. But no marriage succeeds in isolation. We all need help.

Finding mentors

Oh, we humans are so vain. We all want to look good, so it's amazing how we try to keep up the pretense that everything is under control, even when we're completely confused and sinking fast.

It takes a mature and confident person to say, "I need help." That may sound like a contradiction, because we think of mature people as not being "needy," but *having a need* is not the same thing as being weak or incompetent. On the contrary, it is a sign of strength and wisdom when a person is able to look at a situation and say, "This is more than I can handle on my own."

Although each couple's situation is unique, the two of you do have enough in common with the rest of humanity that it is possible for older, wiser, "been there, done that," happily married couples to help you.

The only sensible thing to do is find the people who know how to be happily married and who can explain it to you so you can be happily married, too.

You can regard this season of your life as an opportunity to find some really excellent people.

Let's suppose you wanted to plant a flower garden. You might look up and down your street to see what your neighbors have done. Would you go talk with the neighbor whose yard was a tangle of weeds and dog doo-doo, or would you consult with the neighbor whose garden is a beautiful display all year round? That doesn't take a lot of pondering, does it? So why should it be any different when you are cultivating the "garden" of your marriage?

And I'm not talking about people who have stayed married for a long time. Marriage is not purely a matter of endurance or sheer longevity. There are, unfortunately, couples who will never get divorced but who will never know the joy and peace of a good marriage. It's sad. I've seen elderly couples walking through the supermarket mocking each other and calling each other names. Horrible. I cannot imagine the awful life such people have spent together.

I urge you to find couples who know how to be happily married. I'm talking about that white-haired couple who still hold hands. He calls her his "bride," and she honors him lovingly. They have a glow about them that speaks of a life well spent, and they seem to know a great secret about caring for one another.

What? You say you don't know anyone like that? Then it's time to start looking! Here's the thing: I didn't know anyone like that either, but they are out there, and even better, there are a lot of them who can explain to you how simple it is to have a marriage like theirs.

You read that correctly: I said "simple." I did *not* say "easy." There is a difference. Simplicity is one of the most difficult things for a modern person to achieve. Why? Because every moment of every day, the complexities of life come racing at us, demanding our attention. Do you keep a list of chores and errands? I do, and I'd be lost without it. If we don't make time for the important things of life, the thousand big and little responsibilities we all bear will crowd them out.

So consider where you might find your mentors. You are looking for people who not only hold hands and beam at each other, you need them to be good teachers, people who have the ability to teach marriage skills. Knowing how to do something and being able to teach someone else how to do it are two very, very different skills. We've all seen interviews with long-married happy couples, and they tend to say the same things: "Don't go to bed angry, even if you have to stay up talking all night," and "Think of the other one first," and "Find something to laugh about together every day." It's all good advice, and there is wisdom in it, but there's a world of difference between those good suggestions and the clearly described necessary ingredients that go into a good marriage.

Some churches have groups designed to help young couples with the adjustments they face in the early years of marriage. These may be anything from formal classes to informal social groups who get together with a minimum of guided discussions. There are also weekend seminars in which you go to a hotel or other meeting place and have intensive marriage enrichment activities, and there may be follow-up groups you can participate in. Private counselors may know of other resources, and they may also conduct their own sessions, with couples or groups of couples. And of course, once you become aware that you need guidance, you may realize that you

already know people who might be able to help
you along.

Believe

You've got to trust yourself enough to
believe that the right help is out there and that you
will know it when you find it.

I have a friend who went into a deep,
inexplicable depression in her early 30s. She had a
wonderful husband and two terrific children, but
she didn't want to keep living. She went to a
reputable psychologist regularly for a year but
made no progress against her deep despair. Then
on her own initiative she decided to look for
another counselor, and found one, and the
difference was dramatic. She knew immediately
after the first meeting that she would get to the
bottom of her mysterious depression. She said it
was like getting on the right airplane headed for
the right destination; she put on the seatbelt and
they took off.

My friend, who had never felt the need to
see a counselor in her life before, demonstrated
remarkable persistence. As it turned out, her
problems, as they slowly emerged, were severe,
but ultimately, with the help of good counseling,

she was able to overcome them and lead a happy life. I tell this story to illustrate the importance of trusting your instincts to lead you to the right help. You'll know it when you find it.

One of the ways you'll know that you've found the right counselor or counseling situation is that you will feel peace. That peace won't come because all your problems get solved in the first meeting. In fact, it may be that you will find peace in getting a grasp of just how great the problems are. But somehow, you will sense that there is a path through the woods, and that will be enough. All we need sometimes is the assurance that there *is* a way through, no matter how long the journey. All we need is a little green sprout to know that the garden will grow.

A word of warning: it might sound strange, but there are counselors out there who are "anti-marriage" and seem to end up advising a large percentage of their clients to get divorced. Due diligence is important in choosing the right counselor.

And what if your spouse won't go? Then *you* go, alone. You'll start to feel better, and maybe your spouse will become interested enough to want to find out "what's going on." Sometimes during a season of counseling, the counselor will want to see you alternatively as a couple and then separately.

As to the expense, my husband and I came to regard it as an investment. I remember one occasion when we had $300 in the bank and spent $100 of it to see the counselor, because it was that important to us, and because that much good—peace, understanding, and hope—came out of each session. And there are counselors who will work with you on a sliding scale basis.

Again, needing guidance for your marriage is like needing a dentist. When it hurts, get help.

Chapter Five
I'm too tired to keep trying.
I just want out.

Maybe you've read this far and all you feel is tired.

You keep thinking about what it would be like to be single again; these days it seems that that thought is always in the back of your mind—or maybe even in the "front" of your mind. In fact, it might be that these days the thought of being single again is the only thought that refreshes you—lifts your thoughts and lightens your spirit, so much so that by now it's an idea that's with you on a daily—or maybe hourly—basis. It has become such an attractive thought, a "place" you go in your mind, that now it has reached the point where it seems like the only thing that makes sense.

Yes, you know it will create an enormously messy few months to get through, but most of the time it is as if you are looking beyond a shipwreck and seeing a calm and alluring beach beckoning you. And so you go—mentally—toward that lovely-looking "beach" more and more often.

Sneaking away from home

If I have just described something that you have found yourself doing, I want to warn you that you are creating what may be your biggest problem, because in fantasizing that way, you are mentally abandoning your marriage.

And you *know* that is exactly what you are doing.

If you are an honest person—if you have a conscience, as most people do—you are increasingly uncomfortable over this little "escape mechanism," because you are aware that your thoughts are carrying you farther and farther away from the person you promised to remain close to for the rest of your life. And, as we'll discuss in the chapter on temptation, it's amazing how often life will present you with a real live attractive "alternative" once you've started imagining how life could be if you weren't married.

Creating a new life

The concept that our thoughts create our reality is more than just a great idea for sales seminars. What we tell ourselves about life is what we experience as "reality." That is, we don't experience life directly. Instead, our minds put every new experience through a complex set of "filters" based on our previous experience. We interpret what is happening now based on similar things that happened to us in the past. In everything we go through in life, we don't directly perceive what is happening; we instead *tell ourselves about* what is happening.

And many people today start telling themselves that "what is happening" is the end of their marriage, when that is not at all what is happening.

Tell yourself the truth

We like to think that our modern lives are so challenging that no one has ever had the same level of difficulties that we have. But marriage is not more difficult now than it ever was before. The only difference between "the old days" and now is that divorce has lost its shame, so more people let "tough times" break them apart.

Previous generations faced the same sorts of challenges in marriage that current generations do, but instead of telling themselves, "This is the end of our marriage," many more of them told themselves, "These are the normal stresses and strains of life." Then they went about the business of living through those normal stresses and strains, and they learned to work things out. Their methods of coping might have been good, bad, or indifferent, but they coped. They talked things out, complained, fought, or laughed together at their troubles, and they had marriages that stayed whole and gave them various degrees of satisfaction, depending on how well or how badly they dealt with the challenges. And of course there are millions of couples today who have that same ability to face the tough stuff and work it out.

But these days so many others come up to those same challenges and just quit. Where previous generations saw bumps in the road, current generations see solid brick walls that cannot—or need not—be surmounted. People speak about "moving on," as if it is the best and most natural response to almost any problem, large or small, that they may encounter in marriage.

There are reasons why current generations don't have the same "stick-to-it-ive-ness" that their grandparents did.

One of the main reasons is that there are a lot more possibilities open to people in this country than there have been for any people, ever, in human history. The past few generations of ordinary Americans created and enjoy a level of general prosperity that has never before been seen anywhere in the world. More people at more levels of the economic scale have had access to abundant food, clean water, comfortable housing, and free education than any culture has ever before been able to create. The concept that every human being has the right to personal fulfillment—the right to "life, liberty, and the pursuit of happiness"—was the engine of this prosperity.

But then in the middle of our great prosperity, something happened: personal fulfillment became equated with personal happiness, and personal happiness became an obsession. As a result, we walk around believing that we have an *absolute right* to be happy *all the time*, and if we are not, well then, we had better take stock and figure out who or what is to blame for this unacceptable condition. We must find the source of our unhappiness, and eliminate it, whatever it is, from our lives. And very often— what a surprise!—the "problem" is the person we're sharing our life with.

Women in the modern world have far more possibilities open to them than women have ever had anywhere on earth at any time in history. Women in the modern world are not beholden to men for their upkeep—not financially dependent, as previous generations have been. Unlike women in other times and places, a married American woman who doesn't like her situation doesn't have to tolerate it. Unlike women in other cultures who have had no means of surviving outside the marriage, she can leave her marriage and work to support herself, if she wishes.

Shame, shame

Getting divorced used to be something people were ashamed of. When I was a little girl in the 1950s, my grandmother's brother divorced his wife, and it was shocking. It was awful. It was as if something horrible had happened to the whole family. "Divorce" used to be a word that people whispered behind their hands. A person who was divorced had a big question mark over his or her head.

These days it seems there is hardly anything left that people feel ashamed of.

If we could, would it be a good thing to go back to that way of looking at divorce? No. But today's rather casual attitude is not the right thing, either, especially where children are concerned. I am horrified at the number of smart people I know who are absolutely clueless about what their divorces and the fallout from their divorces are doing to their children.

I understand that divorce is painful, and that pain is exhausting, and pain makes people self-centered. I understand that people in the middle of divorce are confused and lonely. But it makes me nuts when divorcing parents express exasperation because their hurting, angry, confused and lonely children are behaving badly.

I feel, therefore I am

Another aspect of our modern lives that tends to make us give up on marriage is the way people rely on their feelings and emotions. Recently I heard of a woman who left her husband after several years of marriage because she realized she "just didn't love him anymore." A friend of mine said, in the middle of a divorce, that she reached a point where she could not think about reconciliation, because she didn't *feel* anything for her husband any more.

These women are not stupid. My friend has years and years and years of higher education. Yet these women believe that what they *feel* is the final test of whether they should toss over their marriages.

I'm not sure where, when, or why *feelings* became such a dominating force in people's lives, but I suspect it was my generation, the baby boomers, that did it. Heaven knows we led the world off track in plenty of other ways. Those of us who came of age in the hippie-dippy era certainly made "feelings" the ultimate measure of worth. One of the most famous sayings of that age was: "If it feels good, do it." That's a fine saying to live by if we're talking about changing your nail polish color, but leaving a marriage because of the way it "feels" is not the path of wisdom.

Your feelings toward your spouse are going to change radically over the years. We women, who experience several decades of roller-coaster emotions due to the monthly hormonal changes of our menstrual cycles, are vulnerable to wild swings in emotion, but men, too, are liable to be carried away. In fact, in some ways men can be more vulnerable than women because in our culture, men are not allowed a lot of outlets for the powerful emotions that they feel. A man who has grown up denying his emotional needs may be completely overwhelmed when, for example, a flirtatious co-worker makes a move on him at a time when he is feeling unloved and unappreciated at home.

We cannot completely control our feelings. They change like the weather. In the course of a day, I may feel overcome with tenderness toward my husband, annoyed by something he has done, guilty over something he asked me to do that I didn't do, or hotly romantic. I am free to feel whatever I feel toward him, because the basis of our relationship is an unchanging commitment— we *will* love one another. That's our *behavior*. We have resolved to treat each other with respect, affection, and loving concern.

People who believe that their emotions are the center of their beings, the "final court of appeal" for their decision-making in the conduct of their lives, are going to change spouses the way other people trade in their cars—or at least they'll want to!

The love account

I said that my husband and I have agreed to behave lovingly toward each other. That was not an easy thing to do. In our early years together, we built up a big deficit as far as the way we treated each other, and not only was it hard to make up that deficit, it felt really weird once we started.

Our problem wasn't that we fought, because we didn't fight a lot. I was a very angry person, and I'd say terrible things to my husband, but he didn't defend himself or get angry in response. Instead, he'd retreat. And of course, that would only make me much more angry. (Does any of this sound familiar to you?)

I don't think about those bad old days very often, but when I do, it amazes me that we got through. We really didn't have a clue.

Oh, and, by the way, fighting—or "having a loud discussion" as someone once called it—isn't necessarily bad. Some couples actually work things out quite satisfactorily that way. It is their style, and they don't consider it a negative quality in their relationship. But of course, there are ways to "fight fair" that don't destroy the other person or the relationship.

Making it work

So here you are, and maybe you've said and done some things to each other that you think you'll never be able to make up for. It feels artificial and kind of silly to think about starting to say and do things that are sweet and kind and supportive, because you think you've already shown your spouse your "true" self and your "real" feelings.

Well, get over it. Both of you have probably said and done stupid things, but so what? Remember, you're a deeply flawed individual who has a lot of growing to do. So welcome to the human race. Can you forgive yourself? Can you forgive that person over there who promised to love your deeply flawed self?

If you're going to make it work, you have to start rebuilding sometime, and today is as good a day as any.

Nobody else is going to come into your home and fix this for you. If you want money in the bank, you'll have to start putting some money into your account. If you want love at home, you'll have to start putting love into your home.

If you don't know how to do that, admit it.
Now admit it to each other.

Hey, now you're starting to get the idea!

Chapter Six
The Spiritual Connection

If you read the introduction to this book, *which you were supposed to do before you got this far*, you know that this is not a "Christian" book in the sense that it is intended only for Christian readers.

But there is a lot of practical wisdom in living according to Judeo-Christian principles, not just for marriage, but for living a good life, no matter who you are and what you are doing. People who live according to the guidelines of their faith enjoy higher degrees of physical and mental health, all-around fulfillment, and contentment with their lives. So it's just plain common sense to practice your faith (or to continue your spiritual search if you have not found a satisfactory answer yet).

What's God got to do with it?

I grew up in a household where there was no evidence of spiritual awareness. Zero, zip, zilch. My large extended family had a strong Jewish identity, but it was an ethnic, cultural identity, rather than anything to do with God. God was not in the picture in our home, except for those occasions when we children were behaving badly. At those times, we were assured that God was "watching us," and He would punish us for our actions. I got the mental picture of an angry God standing with His arms folded across His chest, just waiting for the opportunity to "zap" me. There was never any indication that He liked, let alone loved, any of us.

From my early teens through my early 20s I searched for a connection with God, but I never found it. I went to various synagogues and churches, and something always happened to turn me off. At some point I gave up, forgot about it, put it in the back corner of my mind as something naïve and immature that I had outgrown.

Then I moved to a city that was having a huge spiritual explosion. Boulder, Colorado, was a center of "alternative lifestyles," and it seemed that everyone was on his or her own fascinating religious/spiritual kick. I abandoned myself to whatever spiritual "flavor of the month" I was around, and there were plenty of weird flavors available—all kinds of traditions from around the world, most of them from non-Western cultures. I was someone snacking at a buffet table, sampling a little magical stuff here and a little mysterious stuff there, but never settling in to commit myself wholeheartedly to a sit-down meal. In being so detached, I thought of myself as "free," and I regarded people who followed one faith tradition, especially an "old-fashioned" Jewish or Christian tradition, as closed-minded, judgmental, and unsophisticated.

My husband had grown up attending the mainline-denomination Protestant church in which his parents were elders, but again, there was no strong sense of a loving, present God in his home, either. When he reached his teen years, he drifted away. (And when my in-laws got divorced because my father-in-law was involved with another woman at their church, that put the finishing touch on our contempt for "organized religion.")

By the time my husband and I met each other, it had been several years since either of us had given any thought to a spiritual commitment. I don't think we would have even understood what that phrase meant. It would have been an alien concept for us at that time. As far as our relationship went, all we knew was that we were completely infatuated with one another.   We considered ourselves reasonably intelligent, and we shared a similar sense of humor. We were very comfortable together; we could talk for hours and hours and never get bored. I saw that he was an extraordinary person, and I felt incredibly lucky not only to have found him, but that he felt the same way about me. What more could you ask for? After just a few weeks, we acknowledged to one another that we were "in love."

So we started life together. We never discussed anything to do with God, and we never talked about church. It simply wasn't a part of our lives. We were in the middle of a time and place in which the elements of "hippie" culture reached their height, and in our social circle, there was the sense that everything regarding spirituality was really cool—except, of course, anything to do with traditional Judeo-Christian beliefs. There was a great variety of world religions being espoused all around us. We were open to just about anything and everything—so much so that we never even considered that we needed to take any further steps than simply enjoying the passing parade of beliefs. To us, "being spiritual" meant whatever we wanted it to mean. We were going to be kind, and peace-loving, and generous whenever we wanted to be.

Wonderful, wonderful me

Among our friends at that time, there was only one obligation that we acknowledged: the obligation to be fulfilled in one's own self. Personal development was all that mattered. Self-fulfillment was the goal—self-fulfillment was the god, in fact. Remember, we whole-heartedly subscribed to the notion that, "If it feels good, do it." And if self-fulfillment meant that a person left his or her marriage and abandoned his or her children, well, so be it. It didn't matter who else got hurt in one's own quest for spiritual wholeness. All that mattered was that a person made himself or herself happy.

And so, ironically, the spiritual search of my generation ended up with many of us living a self-centered, self-absorbed existence in which pleasure was the greatest good. We gave lip service to a sort of earth-worship, nature-worship spirituality, but for me at least, life was all about trying to feel good, and I kept my options open and kept jumping from one interesting new philosophy to the next.

"I do"—for now

When it came to marriage, this guiding premise—we'll do whatever we want to do that feels good—was the basis of the relationship.

One of the "new ideas" that came out of this silly season was the concept of "open marriage"—when either member of a married couple could pursue any number of additional romantic relationships while staying married. Yeah, that was a brilliant concept. It's embarrassing to remember that some of this stuff seemed to make sense at the time.

Lots of our friends wrote their own "creative" marriage vows, including one couple who promised to stay together "as long as we both shall *love*." And that phrase captures the whole spirit of that age, the whole mistaken idea we had about love: whatever "love" was, when it went away, it was time to quit the relationship. When people didn't *feel the love* any more, why should they stay in something that wasn't good for either of them?

"Love," the way we saw it then, was entirely based in our emotions of the moment. Today I'm crazy about you. Tomorrow I like you a lot. The next day I'm crazy about you again. The day after that, I'm really upset with you, and I'm starting to wonder about you. The following day, you really let me down, and now I'm starting to fall out of love. Can't you try harder to make me love you?

Yeah, as if that's a recipe for lifelong marriage. But that was our understanding of love, and that would have remained our understanding had we not met people who could show and tell us what love really was.

Stumbling into the Kingdom of God

When I was 34 years old, I met a man who extended a simple invitation to me. He asked me to consider the possibility that God is real, that His name is Jesus, and that I needed Him.

Praying with this man, I opened to that possibility, and at that moment, the Lord became real to me. I cannot explain how it happened. The writer C. S. Lewis described something similar. He was a passenger on his brother's motorcycle. They were riding to a local zoo. He wrote, "When we set out I did not believe that Jesus Christ was the Son of God, and when we reached the zoo I did."

That's all there was to it. One minute Jesus was far away from my life, and the next, He was present, real, alive, and the Son of God.

Abundant grace

Remember, I was accustomed to being around "spiritual people," and I had dabbled in a couple of other religions. So I didn't think all that much about what had happened. I had not been on a spiritual quest. I had responded to the man's invitation in a sort of "why-not, what-the-heck" moment. I prayed with the nice man, and went home. And everything of my life, from that day to this one, was transformed.

From that first day, I didn't feel alone and desperate any more. I felt calm. Our apartment, which had been a dark and unhappy place, now seemed bright and cheerful.

I had always been a person who liked to talk about changes in my life, and whenever I found something that was good for me, I wanted to persuade other people that it was good for them, too. Now I was enjoying keeping quiet. I told my husband about how good I felt, but I didn't feel as if he needed to go on this journey with me. I was never afraid of what might happen if he didn't share this.

And I didn't rush off to church. I didn't even read the Bible. I felt patient—and that was way, way new to me. I needed to take my time with whatever was going on, and I felt as if I *could* take my time with this, to check it out. There was no pressure from anywhere—not from inside, not from anyone outside. I stayed with the sense of this inner change, and waited to see if "it" was still there each day.

And it was there, day after day.

Over those days and weeks, my husband observed the profound change that had occurred in me, and then he too, opened to the possibility that Jesus was something more than the forgettable Jesus of his church upbringing.

We started going to church. And we met people there who were happily married, and what's more, they could teach us how to be happily married, too. And they did. And now my husband and I tell other people about what we learned.

Keep searching

If you have had times in your life when people have talked to you about taking a "step of faith" and you didn't respond, don't give up on yourself, and don't give up on your search. I had plenty of occasions when well-meaning people—including lots of clergymen!—turned me off. I don't know why something finally "clicked," but if it happened for me, it can happen for you. Don't give up!

I now pronounce you...

Who performed your wedding ceremony, and how did you choose that person?

For many couples, there is an obvious answer: their ceremony was performed by a clergyman who has an important place in the life of the bride, the groom, or both.

But when people come from two different religious backgrounds, they will often make some adjustment; for example, they may have a representative of each tradition officiate, or they may have chosen one or the other.

Sometimes when there is a difference of backgrounds, or when there is no connection to a tradition on either side, a judge may perform the ceremony.

Whom God hath joined together...

However, there are also people who have no strong connection to a faith tradition, but somehow they have a strong desire to put a nice "religious finish" on their vows.

Was that you?

Come on.

Be honest. Did you have a church wedding because of your deep conviction that your marriage was a covenant made between the two of you before God, or did you marry in a house of worship because you liked the idea of putting a spiritual "shine" on the occasion?

Please don't feel like I'm accusing you of something wrong! There's no shame in it. Plenty of people ignore their spirituality until the "big ticket items" of life loom on the horizon: marriage, birth, death. I was that way for years and years, and the way I see it, that only proves that, no matter how much we ignore spirituality in our everyday lives, we *know* deep down that there is something real about it.

See you in church?

So...have you set foot in a house of worship since your wedding?

I'm not trying to make you feel guilty or bad if you haven't.

Unfortunately, belonging to a church or synagogue doesn't seem to make a bit of difference in the success or failure of a marriage, because, sadly enough, there is no difference in the divorce rate among people who practice their faith and those who don't. So if your wedding was the last time you entered a house of worship, please don't think I am pointing a finger at you. If there is any finger-pointing to be done, it would be pointed toward the religious institutions that are not providing sufficient resources to help people build solid, fulfilling, divorce-proof marriages.

In fact, if you went to a church or synagogue for your wedding even though you have not followed a faith tradition before or after that occasion, I applaud you for wanting to "do it right" by being married with the Lord's blessing.

And truly, you did do it right, because every gesture of acknowledgement of the Lord is the right thing to do.

I only want to encourage you to continue to seek, to look for a local congregation to be your "home," because there can be enormous strength and support available in being part of a spiritual community.

Please understand that I'm the last one to try to "shove religion down your throat." It took me half a lifetime to find a home church. And I clearly remember how, until I was ready, I found any kind of evangelism deeply offensive, because when people push you toward a spiritual commitment, it seems to suggest that you are somehow incomplete or insufficient as a person— and not part of the "in crowd."

So if you have read this far and you're starting to think I have tricked you into some kind of "God infomercial," that is not my intent. Yes, we all know stories about people getting "burned" by religion, or "going off the deep end," but that's the human side of the equation. Anywhere you find people you're going to find complications and craziness. You're never going to find a congregation that is pure and free of trouble. But you can find a congregation where you will feel welcome, appreciated, supported, loved, and helped. There are a lot of people out there who know how to be happily married and can explain the steps to take so you can be happily married too. The only place I ever met these people was in church, and that's the only reason I'm recommending that you look there yourself.

Giving your life away

So, what *did* happen when you got married in a house of worship? Well, whether you intended to do so or not, you stood at that altar and gave God permission to use your spouse to mold and shape you into the person He desires you to be. That is, we declare that we are each going to be the agent of change—that is, improvement—for the other, more than anyone else will be in life; we are willing to become instruments in God's hand for making each other better people than we could ever become on our own.

And you thought you were just making nice in front of God.

Ouch, that hurts

So if we're actually giving our lives to each other when we marry, it stands to reason that we are going to experience changes.

Raise your hand if you enjoy changes.

I thought so.

Me neither.

We should not be surprised when there are times that this process is painful. Getting to know another person on a daily basis, sharing a home, and then not just dealing with another person's unique personality, but coming face to face with our own weirdness, well, these adjustments are often difficult. Basically, when a person gets married, he or she disrupts an entire lifetime's worth of habits and behaviors. Disruptions are often annoying, or just plain uncomfortable. I assume you've discovered some of the "annoying" and "uncomfortable" parts, which is why you're reading this book.

I wasn't expecting it to be like this

Being married means putting your spouse first. Were you ready for that? I know I wasn't. Remember that we live in a culture that teaches us to "look out for number one." Marriage works best when we think less about "number one" and more about "the *other* one," and in a culture that does not put the least bit of value on self-sacrifice, the demands of marriage can start to seem almost ridiculous. And of course, we all tend to be self-centered anyway, so the world is not "feeding" us anything different from our own nature.

I'm for you, honey

We must become our spouse's biggest fan if we are to succeed. We have to learn how to give, how to *for*give when our spouse has done something really stupid, and how to build each other up at the end of a day after the world has kicked the stuffing out of us. Through all these lessons, we ultimately learn how to make home a haven where, no matter what the world does to us or what dumb stuff we do during the day, there is someone who always thinks the best of us and wants the best for us.

Spiritual food

Looking for the best in someone, giving constant support and encouragement, and not complaining—I don't know about you, but I am not naturally inclined to do such things. I had to learn. In fact, first I had to *un*-learn a lot of bad responses. I was an angry, scared woman with a wicked tongue. I could destroy my husband in an instant with the things that came into my head and out of my mouth.

The kind word, the selfless act of service, the generous gift—nope, that would not be me if I were left on my own. Again, I don't think I'm that much worse than most people. Without training and reinforcement, raw human nature is not lovely. If you have spent any time around two-year-olds, you know that no one has to teach a child how to be a brat. Bad behavior—that rotten, two-year-old's selfishness—seems to come naturally to all of us.

It was at church that I began to learn how to be a wife worth coming home to. It wasn't just the sermons. It was the people of the congregation whom we met, who told us their own stories of the things they had to learn in order to make their marriage "heaven on earth." And they invited us into their homes, so we could see "living sermons"—what the teachings looked like when they were put into practice. And they looked mighty good to us.

It took us a while, but we did get good at loving each other, and these days my husband and I are assuring young couples that they can make their homes pretty heavenly places, too.

As I mentioned at the beginning of the chapter, study after study has shown that people who maintain a spiritual connection live longer, happier, healthier lives.

So I encourage you, if you haven't found a congregation where you feel "at home" yet, keep looking. The spiritual part of a human being needs daily nourishment every bit as much as the physical part does. Have you been starving yourself to death?

Chapter Seven:
Children:
Yes? No? Maybe?
Or: Yours, Mine, and Ours

But I want a baby!

Let's start with those of you who don't have children yet.

If, during your engagement, the two of you discussed having children, and decided on a time to get pregnant, and the time is "now," and your "biological clock" is ticking away like mad, you're probably feeling an enormous amount of tension these days. You're aware that it's not a good idea to get pregnant while you are questioning the survival of your marriage, and yet....

Yes, time is slipping by, and you may be thinking that if you wait much longer, you may never have children at all. But bringing an innocent life into the middle of an unstable situation is about as selfish as it gets, and parenthood is—or should be—all about self*less*ness—putting your own needs aside in order to do what is best for your child.

The desire to have a child is built into us, and it had better remain that way, or the human race will become extinct! But fulfilling that yearning is not going to make the rest of your marriage turn blissful. In fact, the stress of raising children is quite hard on a marriage. A crying baby at 2 AM is just the beginning of about twenty years of giving, giving, and more giving. You had better put your marriage in good order first.

But maybe what we really need is a child…

Let's get that horrible idea out of the way immediately: having a baby will *not* be the cement that holds together a shaky marriage. (Think of it this way: if you already feel "stuck," adding cement is not going to help!)

A couple of generations ago, having a baby was the standard "cure-all" advice for the marriage blues. In fact, that's how I came into this world: after a year of marriage, my mother wanted to leave my father. A well-meaning physician told her that what she *really* wanted was to have a baby, and so I was born. Four years later my sister came along because my father didn't think it was right for me to remain an only child, and that was the way my parents created our family.

After 25 years, my parents divorced. Technically, I suppose you could say that having children had held them together. But their marriage was not fulfilling to either of them. My parents never did learn to live together peacefully, and they both had adulterous entanglements; my mother's affair began while she was pregnant with my sister and lasted through my entire childhood.

The perfect marriage

I am *not* saying that you need to resolve absolutely every issue between you and your spouse before your marriage is on solid enough ground for raising children. You're in desert-dry conditions right now, and you do need help, but, just like planting a garden, if you work on your relationship, feeding and watering, then the day will come when you'll recognize the emerging "green sprouts" of renewed hope and joy. Trust yourselves enough to believe that you two will recognize the time when you are ready to provide a solid, peaceful, loving home for a child.

I know we talked about having children, but...

Let's back up for a moment: I mentioned that the two of you may or may not have discussed having children. Before you got married, *did you* talk seriously about whether or not you wanted to have children? Did you have a time frame in mind, or certain financial goals you wanted to reach before starting a family?

If you discussed this life-changing decision only in the vaguest terms—"I-guess-I-want-kids"—then you definitely need to discuss it in more detail. But even if you recognized how important this would be to your future together, and discussed it deeply, studied it thoroughly, and thought you knew exactly what your decision would be, well, things change, don't they? We can never know precisely what we are going to feel in a particular situation until we are in the middle of it. In marriage, in living together, in experiencing the ups and downs of daily life with another person, what we might have thought we understood about our life together may prove to be quite different from what life together really turns out to be.

A change in attitude will trigger a whole new "re-negotiation" of what we had agreed on beforehand. So, what happens when one is ready but the other is not? Or, even more perplexing, what happens when you thought you were in agreement about having children at all, but now one of you has had a change of heart?

Or perhaps you talked in the most general terms about having children "one day," and now the "day" has come for one of you, but not the other.

Oh, there are so many ways this issue can blow up in our faces!

Maybe you both wanted children right away, but haven't been able to conceive.

Maybe you were in total agreement about waiting for a few years, but the baby came anyway.

Maybe one of you had children who were living with a former spouse, and now the children want to come live with you.

Only one thing is for sure: once you have children, you have them, so it's pretty much a one-way street as far as that decision.

And don't kid yourself: no matter how mature and settled a person may be, everybody has moments when the responsibility of raising a child seems overwhelming. (But that's only because it *is* overwhelming.)

Tick, tock, tick, tock....

You wouldn't plant a beautiful rose bush in the middle of a vacant lot full of weeds, broken glass, and old abandoned cars, would you? Then stop thinking about bringing a beautiful baby into a home that is the emotional equivalent! Deal with the relationship issues first, because settling your relationship issues is the foundation for everything else you want in life in terms of raising a family. Don't fall for the deception that it will take too long to work things out and you will be too old to have children. It's way better for a child to have a happily married mother or father who is 35 or 40 than a miserably married—or divorced—one who's 28.

I'm ready but he/she isn't

Some marriages are thrown into crisis when one spouse decides "it's time" to have a baby, and the other one doesn't agree.

Isn't it awesome to think that we are among the first human beings on earth who have ever had the luxury of having a *choice* as to whether or not to have children? Starting in the middle of the 20th century, couples have been able to decide not only *if* they wanted children, but *when*, and *how many*.

For all of human history up until then, children just came along—or didn't. We are among the first generations of humanity for whom having children is a matter of choice.

But it is not always wonderful to have the option of making a conscious choice in life. Although we humans love the idea of having control over our lives, the reality of making decisions can, and does, create an enormous amount of anxiety.

How is your kitchen? Do you dream of a complete kitchen "make-over"? Does it seem as if it would be a lot of fun, choosing everything so it's just the way you want it? Then I suggest you talk with someone who has just remodeled a kitchen. Or, ladies, how about your wedding plans? Did you enjoy every moment of making those choices? Or did you, like most people, reach a point where you were tired of all the choices, where you had lost sight of the "big picture," and you felt as if your brain could not contain one more possibility for flowers or the cake or the veil or…whatever.

The decision as to whether to obligate the remainder of one's life to a child or children is probably the most profound choice a human being can make. It's not just a matter of the right paint for the wall or the right flowers for the bridesmaids. It's real life, for the rest of your life. Maybe you've looked forward to it for your whole life up until now, or maybe you're just scared spitless of the whole thing and your spouse is pushing to go ahead with it.

If you're living in that anxiety right now, and that anxiety seems to be wrecking the peace and pleasure of your marriage, this is another instance in which a counselor can help you explore the thoughts and emotions around this decision. Remember that you are not the first couple to come to this crossroads, and there are skilled counselors who can guide you through the process.

And remember, too, that it is a good sign, a sign of your maturity, that you are hesitating before you make this enormous decision. By all means, examine yourselves.

Most of all, remember that all of life's decisions are trade-offs. That is, there will be a "plus" column and a "minus" column on each side of the issue. It won't be as simple as picking the longer list and going for it, but it will help you both think clearly if you recognize that there are benefits and drawbacks to a life with children, and there are benefits and drawbacks to having a life not having children.

When you've taken the time to discuss the situation, you'll be able to make a choice that will bring you peace.

We're both ready, but…

What if you both want a child very much but can't get pregnant?

Bernie and Amy went through it. Bernie said, "People think it must be 'fun' to try to get pregnant, because they imagine that you are making love all the time. But when you're trying to conceive, your sex life becomes a sort of medical procedure rather than a spontaneous expression of affection and intimacy." Bernie and Amy adopted one son, and conceived the other through in-vitro fertilization—which required four attempts.

Hal and Helen had tried unsuccessfully to get pregnant for 14 years. I have never met two people who wanted children more than they did. Helen had a college degree in early-childhood education, and longed to have a child in their home. Finally, they looked into adoption, and in due time Melanie became their little girl. Several years later, Deanna became Melanie's little sister.

Helen embraced motherhood with a joy that inspired everyone she knew.

Would you, could you, should you adopt? That is something that should be thoroughly discussed and examined. It is awesome to me that people take that step—talk about making a conscious choice! I will say that the experience of raising a child is the important part of "having children." Pregnancy and childbirth are interesting phenomena, but they are not what "being Mom" is really all about. Loving a little one, and letting that love transform and shape your life, is what's important.

Why did I do this?

Now, for those of you who already have a child or two:

Isn't it amazing how having that baby changed everything?

You entered into a whole new world, and very little of what used to be "your life" exists any more.

And there isn't anything about it that is what you expected it to be, is there? Maybe you had the same picture I did: a smooth progression of day upon day of sweet contentment.

No, for most of us, the delight and fulfillment of having a baby comes in brief, unexpected, fleeting moments in the middle of a lot of physical and mental exhaustion and a whole lot of dirty diapers. Starting a family is wonderful, and greatly to be desired. But we're back at that old reality: it's for grown-ups. Everything that used to be front-and-center in your life has been pushed to one side, and in its place is a small, helpless creature who has destroyed every night's sleep for months, and stained your favorite sweater besides. (Oh yeah, and that terrific sex life you once enjoyed seems to have disappeared for good.)

And your mind! What has happened to your mind?! You used to be an interesting person. You were involved in the outside world. You used to *do* things. You were interested in big events and big ideas. Now you spend that last hour of consciousness each evening watching the least mentally challenging TV show you can find.

Once upon a time you kept up with fashions in clothing and hair. Now you're happy if you have something to wear that isn't discolored with something baby-related, and all you require of a hairdo is that it should be something that can be washed and dried in a minute and a half. And jewelry, ladies? Forget it. After a few excruciating earring- or necklace-pulls, jewelry went back into the drawer and stayed there. (I'm told by a reliable source that Daddy's chest-hair-pull is even more painful.)

There was a time when you knew something about music and movies. Now it seems the world is passing you by. You don't have a lot to talk about with friends who don't have children, and while you have a lot to share with the ones who do have children, the most meaningful conversations you seem to have concern your latest visit to the pediatrician, or questions about potty training.

Is it "an adjustment" or a total upheaval?

So you're not alone. All of us end up a little shocked at the way having a baby affects our lives. Nobody is "ready" for it. There's no way you can be. For those of us who gave birth, just the physical changes are profound. Our hormones go nuts for a couple of years—even more nuts than the regular monthly changes. Our bodies stretch out beyond belief, and then kinda sorta go back into shape, kinda sorta. Our poor husbands stand by and watch, and most of the time, have to stifle their own emotional responses to the changes we go through. Oh, and then there's the small matter of having a little stranger come into your home and change everything else.

It should probably not be a surprise that a marriage would "hit the wall" at pretty much the same time as that little bundle from heaven arrives. The emotions around this "blessed event" can be intense and incredibly confusing. On the one hand, you can't imagine life without that sweet little smiling face, but at the same time, the reality of being tied to that child—and to that child's other parent—for the rest of your life can lead to feelings of desperation. You can start to feel as if you're fighting panic on a daily basis, caught in a mental "loop" that goes around and around, loving your child with an intense kind of love you never knew you were capable of, while at the same time resenting being tied to your situation because of that child, and then feeling guilty for the resentment. Exhausting, isn't it?

Well, you are the first and only person ever to have experienced this sort of thing.

Just kidding!

Again, what we're talking about is very normal, but it is also normal that we find it difficult to acknowledge that this wonderful, miraculous, amazing experience of having a child has any negative aspects. We may think having *any* negative emotions about parenthood means we somehow are not "doing parenthood" correctly. We may think there must be something wrong with us for not enjoying parenthood more. We don't want to seem ungrateful, because "everyone knows" that having a child is a blessing. And we may be afraid to say anything about how we feel, because if we say anything, that will bring all our feelings out in the open, and we're terrified of what would happen if we did that. So we just muddle along as best we can while the emotional pressure builds and builds.

I had an example of this several years ago, in a phone conversation with a friend who was worn out from dealing with her two pre-school-age children. She talked for several minutes about how crazy they were making her. I knew exactly what she was talking about, because I had gone through the same thing a few years earlier when my children were toddlers. I told her I understood her feelings and had had the same kind of physical, mental, and emotional exhaustion when my kids were little. And then a strange thing happened: as I expressed understanding and sympathy, my friend began "back-pedaling" like mad, denying that she was feeling unhappy. No matter what I said after that to try to let her know that she didn't have to feel guilty about her very normal feelings, she steadfastly denied that she felt the way she felt—that is, *the way she had just told me she felt*. It was just too hard for her to face the fact that she had let those feelings out in the open, even if all I was doing was telling her that I had gone through the same thing. The reflection was too hard for her to look at.

We seem to get the idea fixed in our minds that we are supposed to feel only gratitude for our family. We're supposed to be overflowing with happiness all the livelong day. We believe that we must never say anything that makes us seem ungrateful for the little lives that have been entrusted to our care.

But the truth is that sometimes raising children is a difficult, crazy-making, frustrating, exhausting job.

Just before my first child was born, my friend Mary gave birth to her first child, and I couldn't wait to talk with her about it. I went to visit when her daughter was a few weeks old, and I asked her, "Well, how is motherhood?"

In her slow Texas drawl, Mary said, "Well, it's all right I guess. But sometimes I think, 'Why'd I *do* this?'"

So if the pressures of parenthood ever seem overwhelming to you, remember you're not the first one to wonder, "Why'd I do this?"

The good advice that nobody takes

There are two pieces of advice, both of them excellent, that are easy to give, but difficult to put into practice.

The first is this: "When baby naps, Mom should nap." Seems obvious, right? New moms need their rest, so at those times during the day when the child sleeps—sometimes once, sometimes twice a day—it makes sense that Mom should do likewise. Great. The only thing is, I've never known anybody who did it. And that's because baby's nap time is usually the only time a mother has to herself, and she wants to *get something done*, even if it's just sitting quietly reading a magazine. (And usually it's more like folding the laundry or cleaning the bathroom.)

The second piece of advice is also worthwhile, and I'm not sure how many people actually follow through on it. People will tell you, "You have to *cultivate* your marriage relationship once you have children. You have to get away from the house, get away from the baby, be alone, just the two of you, and remember your romance."

Now, in case you hadn't noticed, everything about having a baby is intense. The emotions, the physical demands, the total disruption of everything else in daily life—all of it turns your world upside down and inside out.

It is easy for a couple to lose each other in the process of adjusting to becoming a father and mother. You used to have every evening alone together, and the whole weekend to yourselves. You used to have enough energy to do things together. Now time and energy are scarce commodities.

So reminding a couple to get away and give time and attention to each other is great advice, but putting it into practice may seem like more effort than is humanly possible. And another thing: when my kids were small, the awareness of "being Mom" was always there, whether the kids were around or not. When my husband and I did get away for an afternoon or evening, it felt awkward at first, as if we were abandoning our obligations, or maybe, as if we were denying our identities as "Mom" and "Dad." And often it was hard, for the first hour or so, to find something to talk about that wasn't child-related.

My husband and I were not especially good at having "date nights." Other couples we know seemed to be able to get away more easily, for several reasons. We lived far from our extended families, and so we didn't have an eager grandmother or auntie ready to take our kids for a day or an overnight. And we were so broke in those years that having enough money to go out for a romantic dinner was a rarity. And maybe you don't have those resources, either. It is still good advice.

By the way, do you remember how to have fun?

I didn't.

I took motherhood so seriously that the whole idea of "having fun" was not on my radar. Part of it was just my personality and my background. I'm basically a serious-minded person, and the responsibility of taking care of a helpless little person was so heavy on me that there was no room in my life for anything lightweight and frivolous.

If anything like that is happening with you, the place to start is in acknowledging that life has become a little too serious. Your answers won't be the same as my answers, but there are answers.

Step-families

All the many issues that involve children—throughout a couple's relationship—require the utmost care and attention, because innocent little lives are involved. But in remarriages involving children—whose lives have already been through the wrenching upheaval of divorce or the death of a parent—special care is required.

Some studies have shown that the divorce rate for second marriages is even higher than the divorce rate for first marriages. It would be entirely understandable. One reason for the higher rate of divorce in second marriages would be that children are often involved, which multiplies the potential for craziness several times over. "Blended family" is an awfully polite way to describe the challenges when several unrelated people are thrown together under the same roof because two of those people have decided to marry one another.

If you are reading this and you are in a second marriage involving step-children, I'm probably not telling you anything you don't already know.   And if you are in your first marriage and there is a child involved, and it looks to you as if divorce will get you beyond the current shipwreck to an island of peace and tranquility, I have just one word for you:

Hah!

Seriously, just because it seems that half the people you know are juggling step-families, that doesn't mean that it's a wise or good thing to do. It certainly doesn't simplify anyone's life—just ask your remarried friends about it.

And in case you thought your first marriage failed due entirely to your first spouse's character failings, a second marriage can be a real shock.

One friend of mine who speaks from experience says, "Whenever I hear the word 'step-anyone,' I know there is pain involved." That puts it exactly right, it seems to me. Divorce and remarriage that involves young—or not-so-young—children is always going to be emotionally, psychologically, and logistically messy. But should it be any wonder that children of divorce—uprooted, displaced, juggling two homes and being required to adjust to a strange adult sleeping with Mom and/or Dad—start to exhibit strange behaviors?

Children don't often know how to express their needs and emotions in words, and so they will "act out" their feelings. If they are angry, hurting, or frightened—which are all natural responses to the changes that divorce and remarriage bring to children's lives—their behavior may be quite unpleasant, and bring dismay to the adults who care for them. A child experiences the same loss and disappointment in divorce that adults do, but the child cannot replace a father or mother the way adults can replace a husband or wife. That is, children of divorce have been dealt an irreplaceable loss, and a wise and mature couple should be prepared to expend an enormous amount of effort and energy in the creation of their step-family. Along the way, there may be seasons when counseling will ease the pain and strain, and there should be no hesitation in seeking this form of help.

The shotgun wedding

And there are those who got married because they got pregnant. Some people seem to be completely untroubled by it, with a sense that they would have married anyway. In some parts of the world, in fact, a man would not marry a woman unless she proved her fertility by becoming pregnant, because in those cultures it is important that a woman be able to bear children.

But in our culture, being pushed along into marriage with a baby on the way can leave you haunted by doubt: would this have been my choice otherwise? If you got married because you "had to," and you now feel trapped, you may wonder if you can ever be happy together.

If I'm talking about your situation, let me say emphatically that yes, you can overcome the feeling of entrapment and go on to find joy together. But I don't have to tell you that you have to muck your way through some garbage to get there. You know what garbage I mean. First of all, you've got to stop telling yourself all day long that you're trapped. You, more than most parents, have that double-minded thing going on, where you love your baby but can't help but wonder where you'd be if you hadn't gotten pregnant.

Well, you'd be somewhere else with some other kind of garbage to get through, that's where, so stop day-dreaming about it.

Maybe you have experienced some regret, and it has occurred to you that there are some pretty good reasons for the standard moral teachings you heard throughout your life, such as the one about waiting until you were married to have sexual relations, hm? You've learned the hard way that people who get married because they *want to* rather than *have to* don't have to deal with the sort of stuff you're going through.

It's not that you wouldn't have had any problems, but you sure would have eliminated a whole bunch of them, and no one understands that better than you, because you're living them.

Looking back, it may seem that life would have been awfully easy if you hadn't gotten married this way.

But sit up and look around and you'll realize that no one's got an easy life. Just read this chapter again and you'll see that *everything* around having children is a challenge in marriage.

And don't look back. You can't change anything. Life goes in one direction—forward—so let's make today the best we can make it, and prepare to make tomorrow even better. You've got the marriage you've got, and that's what you have to work on.

Chapter Eight
Temptation

There is no such thing as a "harmless flirtation," but when a marriage is under strain, outside involvement is an especially loaded issue.

Sometimes it just happens

Is it possible to get mixed up with someone else even when your marriage is happy and fulfilling? Yes. Absolutely. You can get mixed up with someone else without looking for it, and without having any problems at home.

In fact, I can just about guarantee that, at some point in your marriage, each of you will have someone come on to you, at least once. There will always be people "on the make," and there are a lot of those people who prefer to get involved with married people for their own weird reasons.

If you have had someone come on to you since you got married, you probably felt a bizarre mixture of responses. First, let's admit it, it's flattering, and gratifying. After all, whether you're married or single, it's nice to have someone find you attractive. But most of us who have a conscience find it a little scary, and rightly so, because the situation is threatening to the very foundation of our lives.

You may also think that you must have done something—that you consciously or unconsciously sent out some kind of "signal" indicating that you are available—so that you feel guilty and responsible for what is happening.

But you might not have done anything to bring this on. As I just said, for some people, the allure is that you're already married. These people think it's "safer" to get hooked up with someone who is already committed elsewhere because these poor souls enjoy the game of infatuation, and cannot handle anything more serious.

If you're young, your youth itself is a powerful attractant.

If you are in a position of authority or if you are in a position in which you are powerless, either of those can "inspire" someone to put the moves on you.

And sometimes there is no accounting for it for any obvious reason.

So it doesn't matter where it started. The problem is that it exists at all. And it doesn't matter if it's just a fantasy, a full-on affair, or anything in between. If there is someone else on your mind, I don't have to tell you how bad and dangerous it is, because I'm sure you already know you're in trouble, and you probably feel guilty as all get-out.

Good guilt

At least I hope you feel guilty. If you've don't—if you've convinced yourself that cheating is all right because you *deserve a little happiness*, you're heading 100 mph down a dead-end street. That self-pitying, selfish attitude has no place in marriage. And you're not going to be in a marriage very long if you stay in that frame of mind.

Or maybe you're working so hard, mentally, *not* to feel guilty that it's wearing you out. Your mind is in a constant swirl of anger and guilt, and it's incredibly exhausting. It's crazy time inside your head, and you may even start to wonder why your spouse hasn't noticed.

Why anger?

What's the anger all about? Well, part of it is a by-product of the guilt. Here's the thing about guilt: anyone who has the slightest bit of conscience is intensely uncomfortable with feelings of guilt. It's a "hot potato" and we want to hand it off somewhere else so we can get rid of it. So when we feel guilty about something, we often transfer the feelings of discomfort from our own behavior onto the person who is "making us" feel guilty—that is, the person we're betraying.

So what do we do? It may sound weird, but one of the things we do when we feel guilty toward someone is find a reason to blame that person for something—anything!—to   "equalize"   the pressure—to make us feel as if we really don't owe that person anything.

Oh, guilt can be an ugly thing.

We'll do almost anything to try to shift the blame onto our spouse. We'll try to find something that he or she is doing wrong, to make us feel less uncomfortable about our wandering thoughts (or actions), so we don't feel guilty any more. It's not just a matter of justifying your bad behavior by finding the imperfections in your mate. It's a way of putting some distance between the two of you, emotionally, because when you're close you can feel the stabs of conscience more intensely.

You may have reached the point that you have convinced yourself that your spouse has "forced" you to do whatever it is you're doing. That way, it's not that *you* made the decision to start flirting with someone at the office and it's not *your fault* for cheating. Oh, no, not sweet little innocent you. You started flirting because your spouse never made you feel special any more. Or never made scrambled eggs the way you like them. Or didn't take out the trash often enough. It's not your fault. You were driven to it. You were forced into it.

Yeah, right.

You bug me

Very often one of the first indications that someone is cheating is that he or she has become very irritable. Everything seems to be an annoyance. He or she lashes out at things that ordinarily would not be noticed. That's because not only is the guilt eating away at the cheater, but also because the cheater is living in two different worlds, one on the outside, the other on the inside. It's complicated and tiring. The person is literally living two lives at once, doubling the wear and tear. No one can keep it up very easily for any length of time. The irritability that results from living a double life is one of the first signs that a spouse is cheating.

And if I can cheat, so can you

Another phenomenon that happens quite often—and quite logically, I might add—is that the person who is cheating starts to figure, "Hey, if *I'm* feeling this way, my spouse is probably thinking about—or even acting on!—feelings for someone else, too." So, in an interesting twist, the cheating spouse will often accuse his or her mate of being unfaithful! In fact, that kind of accusation is another indication that the accuser is having an affair!

A seductive idea

If your marriage seems to be heading south, it is not at all surprising that you would start looking elsewhere. You may feel terribly guilty about it, or, if you are feeling terribly sorry for yourself, you may start to think that you deserve "a harmless little flirtation," so you may be rather actively cultivating another relationship, guilty feelings or not.

Here's the thing:

You didn't get those adulterous ideas by chance.

They're in the air.

It's not just that there has been a growing sense, over the past couple of generations, that marriage is a disposable commodity, something to enjoy when it's good and throw away when it's not.

No, it's even worse. Our culture has come to the point where we absolutely glorify adultery. Think about the many books and movies over the past 30 years that tell the story of a man or woman, caught in a boring marriage, who finally "awakens" into a deliciously happy affair, and thus blossoms into a beautiful realization of his or her true self.

Oh, please.

If you want to talk about something that's deadly dull, how many times have people fallen for that same old routine: flirtation, adulterous entanglement, and divorce. What a painfully well-trodden, rutted, muddy, mucky, boring road.

But here we are, immersed in a world telling us just the opposite, that marriage is boring and adultery is thrilling. You'd think, from the way it is portrayed in current movies, songs, and books, that just around the corner there is someone with whom there would be no problems, just an endlessly stimulating relationship that would lift us out of the daily humdrum and make us far more fulfilled than the spouse we have now.

It's as American as apple pie

It's a message that plays into the best and worst of us. There is a restlessness about American culture that is a great part of our nation's success. Other cultures have never supported the kind of wide open possibilities for ordinary people that the United States has. We Americans have seen small-town boys grow up to be President. Inventors in basements and garages have become billionaires. We live in a world where something better is always on the horizon. We Americans are ambitious and competitive, and we enjoy the fruits of a competitive marketplace. There is always someone figuring out how to get the best product to the most people for the least amount of money.

The competitiveness of our economic system has enabled most of us to live at a level of prosperity that would absolutely astonish people of a few generations ago. I can only imagine how my great-great-grandmother, who spent her life in a village somewhere in Russia, would respond if she saw my house, with its central heating, its hot and cold running water, its washer-dryer, etc. The definition of "poverty" in the United States would match the definition of "wealth" throughout most of human history, and in many parts of the world today.

And our culture is brand-new on the world scene. Other people-groups rest on centuries of tradition that, for better or worse, keep people in certain roles and expectations for their entire lives. Human happiness does not always figure into their roles. Our nation has made human happiness not just an expectation, but a right.

We expect to be able to change our situation when we aren't happy, and we seek to discard whatever isn't working for us.

But the same dissatisfaction that leads to brilliant innovations that benefit mankind can be brought home and turned into resentment and unhappiness in a marriage.

Thus we silently absorb the message that, just as there is a better car than the one in your garage, there is a better someone "out there" than the one in our bed, and when marriage hits the *inevitable* bumps in the road, we are led to think about changing spouses. It's part of our make-up as modern Americans.

Love vs. independence

Here's another thing about our culture: we all want to be independent. We glorify the rugged individualist, the one who doesn't need anything or anyone. We admire the explorers who set out on their own to tame the wilderness, armed with just a compass and a rifle, trekking through the woods with no human contact for months on end.

We, too, want to be self-sufficient. We don't want to depend on anything outside ourselves to satisfy all our needs. After all, if you depend on someone else for something, and that person lets you down, you're going to be hurt, and maybe even abandoned. That stinks. So why need anybody else?

That's another message that we have all absorbed, and so we all live that way to some degree, and it gets in the way of being able to love.

Especially if your parents divorced, you are likely to have this "one foot out the door" mentality. And the only problem with that kind of attitude is that you're going to be very vulnerable to an adulterous entanglement and probably never going to be able to enter in to the fullness of committed love. (Other than that, it works fine.)

How did I get into this mess?

How does an adulterous relationship happen?

Again, you don't have to be "on the prowl" to get snared. Maybe someone at work whom you never even noticed before says something that catches your attention, or looks at you a certain way, and everything just seems to unfold from there, and it seems so right, so compelling. You feel as if you just can't stop yourself. You feel guilty but you can't help it. It's exciting and fun, and you realize how *old* you were starting to feel, and how *young* you feel around this other person—not just young, but suddenly you feel like someone who has possibilities opening up that you thought were gone from your life. It's all so marvelous, so glamorous. You're drawn along, day after day, into a different world. Your life feels intensified and magical, as if you're starring in a romantic movie.

Hello?

You *are* reading from a script, my friend, and it's not one that has a happy ending. Skip to the last page—the part where your life goes off a cliff.

But a person has needs

Yes, if your spouse treats you like dirt, and someone at work treats you like royalty, it is going to affect you and your marriage. But how much are you going to value your marriage? How much are you going to value yourself as an honorable human being?

I drive an old car. Right now it really looks bad, too, with a chipped windshield and faded paint, and I'm a little self-conscious about it, here in car-obsessed Los Angeles. So I think I'll go next door and start driving my neighbor's brand-new Mercedes, because I'm tired of driving my old car and besides, I never expected my car to get so nasty looking. I deserve better. I'll feel better in that new Mercedes, and I'll look better, and my friends will like it better when I visit and park the Mercedes in their driveway.

Well of course I'm not going to take my neighbor's car. I never have thoughts like that, but I wanted to illustrate a violation of the limits we put on ourselves as law-abiding, moral people in most areas of our lives.

That example illustrates the absurdity of taking something that doesn't belong to us just because we think it's better than what we have.

Now "translate" that to marriage, when we aren't just dealing with man-made laws about stealing, but something even more important—a vow, a spiritual commitment. For most of us, the vows we make in marriage are the only occasion in which we stand in front of witnesses and voluntarily make promises about how we will conduct ourselves.

You may or may not have a *reason* for your adulterous thoughts, imaginings, or actions, but you do not have an *excuse* for cheating. For your marriage vows to have any meaning, *you* must honor those vows. "Keeping yourself only unto" that person whose toothbrush is in the holder next to yours means that you do not give any part of yourself—mental, emotional, physical, *anything*—to another.

Oh, and something else. If you get involved with someone who is willing to cheat on his or her spouse, or if you start cheating on your spouse, what kind of marriage would come of that relationship? Marriage to a cheater.

And you think you've got a tough situation now? Try marriage with a few broken-hearted kids in tow.

Finding someone else is not the answer. And if you've already found someone else, do yourself a favor and end it. If you're fantasizing about someone else, stop now. If you've gone beyond fantasizing and you're actively flirting, stop now. If you're having an affair, stop now. Don't try to "be friends." Don't call "just to talk now and then." Get rid of any little mementos, any little presents, any little reminders. Block, erase, and get rid of any other means of contact. Don't go for coffee where that person will be getting coffee. Don't even talk with a mutual friend who will maintain the connection indirectly. Cut off every pathway that leads back to that person.

It will take a lot of strength to pull away, but you owe it to yourself, to your marriage, to the vows you made. It may feel awful at first, but righteousness will come of this effort.

There are other ways to make yourself feel good. Honest. It's time to find out what those things are. Decide right now that you will do whatever it takes to find joy with that person you promised to share your life with. You can do it. I know you can. You'll never regret that decision.

Back to the future

Depending on how far into Cheatersville you have gone, the road back will be difficult to a greater or lesser degree. But the amazing thing about deciding to do the right thing is that you can end up better than you were before—better than you would have been if you hadn't gone through a tough time! A lot of good can come out of this kind of recovery: if you hadn't had this experience, you might never have had the opportunity to discover and talk about parts of yourself that maybe you didn't even know existed.

I had a really tough time identifying and describing the things I needed from my husband. I didn't know myself—couldn't articulate the things that were important to me. So there wasn't a lot my husband could do to meet my needs! We were really in the dark.

Counseling helped us a lot in that regard. What we learned was that we humans are all basically wired up in pretty much the same way. We need acceptance, we need warmth, we need forgiveness. It's a matter of recognizing what those things look like in daily life that is often a learning process. This is the business of marriage. This is the heart of it. This is learning to love.

This is what marriage should be about—being willing to learn about what love means to you and to the person you married, and being willing to be transformed into a more loving, accepting, forgiving and forgiven person.

Thirty, forty, and fifty years from now it will mean the difference between you looking back on a trail of broken promises and broken relationships, or looking back on a steady, if bumpy, path toward the fulfillment of everything you had hoped for when you got married. The decision is yours.

Chapter Nine
SEX

Now that I have your attention….

And please, tell me that you didn't turn directly to this chapter before you read anything else!

Well, if you did, that's OK, and here's the good news: I can tell you from experience that it is possible to have a great love life, even after years of total nothingness, frustration and despair. Don't give up on yourself or your spouse.

Not that I have any brilliant words of wisdom that will instantly "bring back the magic." All I can do is assure you that what seems dead, gone, and impossible to retrieve can come roaring back, and be more satisfying than you ever imagined.

A wise old friend of mine once said that, when your sex life is good, it is a part of the overall happiness you enjoy together as a married couple. But when it is not good—or in my case, pretty much non-existent—then it is like a toothache: a small part that causes so much pain you pretty much can't enjoy anything.

Human sexuality is, paradoxically, both an intensely powerful and an incredibly delicate component of our beings. Depending upon what each of you brings to marriage in terms of expectations and background, achieving a mutually satisfying physical relationship can be a challenge to a greater or lesser degree, but it always, always, always requires that a couple be open and honest with one another.

Our sex-saturated popular culture has conditioned everyone's expectations. No previous generations have *ever* been exposed—and I do mean "exposed"—to the images and descriptions of sexuality that we have seen, read, and heard in the past 50 or so years. The irony is that, as our culture has become more open about sexuality, we as individuals have also become more confused about its place in our lives. The message in current popular culture is that sex is as natural (and meaningful) as a sneeze. In the span of one lifetime our culture has gone from "saving myself for marriage" to "doing it whenever I feel like it."

But that's not the only problem

When it comes to marriage, there are some other, simpler and more practical realities that might be messing things up.

Spontaneity might be one of those nice romantic notions that has to be discarded when you're in the middle of raising a family. The whole erotic sense of "I looked at him and he looked at me and..." well, you pretty much have to forget that whole scenario if you've got a couple of young—or not-so-young—children. If you are resistant to the idea of having to schedule time for lovemaking, *get over yourself.* If you wait for it to "just happen," you could be waiting for a long time.

Here's another effect from our popular culture: if you don't happen to have a perfectly toned body—and this is especially true for us women—you can be vulnerable to feelings of inadequacy about your attractiveness, which can really interfere with intimacy. One man I know said his wife has such negative feelings about her body (after three kids) that she cannot get past it. Nothing he says to reassure her of her allure seems to make a difference. He once said, "I'm standing there with my tongue hanging out, but she doesn't believe me." Even though, at age 50, she is still one of the most beautiful women I know, all she sees is the few added pounds and the effects of gravity, and she doesn't believe she's still "got it."

I do believe a husband and wife owe it to each other to stay reasonably in shape, and they definitely owe it to each other to keep their bodies clean and sweet. If you do have "issues" about your self-image and know that it is blocking your ability to respond as a lover, call it what it is. Don't suffer in silence!

And of course, be honest with yourself and your spouse if you have become aware that pornography—which is so incredibly available now, as never before in human history—has affected your sensibilities.

As with all problematic aspects of a relationship, nothing changes unless you acknowledge the truth, forgive yourselves and one another for your failures, and set yourselves to make it better. For most of us, maintaining sexual intimacy is a necessary aspect of a functioning marriage.

Let me say it again: nothing is going to change until you do *whatever it takes* to make the situation better. If you have trouble talking about it with each other, start by saying, "It's difficult for me to talk about this."

What's your problem?

One problem I had was what I called "switching gears," especially when I had young children. Being a mom is an indescribable joy, a gift, a wonderment. It is also the time of life when you can totally lose track of yourself while watching-out-for, cleaning-up-after, feeding, and in all other ways caring for a young child or two or three. I always said I would have been a better mother if I could have done it every other day, with the in-between days for myself, so I could, oh, I don't know, have two thoughts to myself.

And there's what I call the elegance of motherhood, when a little person is spitting up on you, and doing other things that require buying stain remover in the large economy size.

For me, a day of motherhood left me feeling like the farthest thing from a hot mama. So when the man I love came home feeling amorous, there I'd be, feeling like an old dishrag. It wasn't even so much that I was tired (which I often was). It was more that I could not figure out how to transition from good-old-Mom, the human rag, to someone capable of the heights of sexual stimulation. I felt a million miles away from sexual intimacy.

This is important:

Ladies, here's some news: our husbands need sex. It's different for them. Think about it in biological terms. When it comes to reproduction, women's sexual organs are warehouses; we're born with all the eggs in our ovaries that we're ever going to have. But guys' sex organs are factories; they're manufacturing all the time. It creates an urgency about their need for sexual expression, and that's a good thing, as far as insuring the survival of the human race. That urgency is nature's way of insuring that babies get made.

And ladies, while it's not unheard of for a woman to want more sexual connection than her husband does, in general, his physical need is greater than yours. And there's this: it's probably his favorite way that you show him you love him. (Ask him, if you dare.)

In conclusion:

There was a time, a very long time, in fact, when I thought that my sex life was over. I would not have believed that I'd be having this much fun in my seventh decade, but there doesn't seem to be an age limit on having an intimate life that is playful, satisfying, and hot, hot, hot.

Don't give up on yourself, and don't give up on your marriage just because this part of your relationship needs help. You're not the first couple and you won't be the last to face this challenge. Decide you're going to persevere. It's so worth it.

Chapter Ten
Now What?

The time has come for you to take action.

Have you acknowledged to one another that you're aware that your marriage is in bad shape? Have you said those words calmly, quietly, without accusation, but with forgiveness, of yourselves and one another? Have you told each other that you are determined that you are going to do whatever it takes to make your marriage better?

It's important to say those things. It's an important first step.

And you can follow through with all the ways people usually "take action," and all of them are worth doing: you can go for counseling, take marriage enrichment courses, go on marriage retreats, start reading books and *doing* all the good stuff you can do, and it will probably help.

But the most important action you can take is the action of changing your attitude and expectations.

And that's something only you can do, within yourself, all by yourself.

Divorce is no longer the shameful thing it was in previous generations, and a lot of commentators think that the lack of shame about divorce these days is one reason that people have less hesitation about breaking up.

In your great-grandmother's day, *nice* people wouldn't dream of doing anything as low-down as destroying a marriage. Back then, divorce was an announcement to the world that *you* were deficient in some way—at the very least, you were deficient in your ability to choose a suitable mate. As a result, fear of "what the neighbors would say," kept a lot of people suffering silently in dismal marriages, and there were a lot of unhappy households with a lot of terrible secrets.

No one wants a return to those days. Human happiness is valuable, meaningful, and profitable. It is also attainable.

One problem we all share, though, is that divorce is so common these days that many of us live in a state of low-level fear, with the constant expectation that *this* situation or *that* difficulty is going to be the "last straw"—the one occasion that leads to divorce. And when you live in that kind of fearful expectation, you start to see bugaboos around every corner. And so, when the honeymoon shine wears off and the normal ups and downs of life occur, instead of having the entirely reasonable expectation of working together to get through whatever difficulty arises, spouses withdraw from one another and start to imagine the worst. And it is just a short step from imagining the worst to making it a reality.

The root of the problem is *not* that you cannot overcome whatever challenges life presents to you as a couple.

The root of the problem is that you are a slave to fear, which magnifies the significance of everyday situations.

Can you alter your expectations? Can you live in the happy expectation that the two of you can work through anything life throws at you? Can you keep an optimistic attitude about the future of your marriage, and conquer the fear of divorce?

Of course you can!

And there is no more important task to take up. Let's put it this way: you'll have to alter your expectations at some point if you're going to succeed at marriage. You have to look at the challenges, resolve to face them and then overcome them, together. You have to look at your unique situation and acknowledge that you both have room for some beneficial growth.

When a child goes to bed and says, "I'm afraid of the dark. I think there's a monster in my room," Dad or Mom comes into the bedroom and turns on the light. Together, they open the closet, poke around, yell to scare away anything that might be hiding in the closet, and close the door. Then they look under the bed, to make sure there are no monsters hanging out there, either. Finally, the child is reassured, and can rest.

The monsters in your closet are not quite as imaginary as the ones in that child's room. But they will lose their power to destroy your marriage if you will poke and prod a little bit, drag them from the dark shadows of your mind out into the light, and face them down. You'll need to be willing to give the process some time and attention, the same way you'd treat a child's fear of the dark recesses of his world.

Hold on to a mental picture of the two of you, old and gray-haired, smiling and holding hands, surrounded by happy, secure, loving children and grandchildren, resting in the knowledge that you learned to love someone with all your heart and for all your life. That picture won't just happen by itself. You both have to want it above all else, to cling to it together, to sacrifice for it. When the inevitable bumps in the road toss you around, you have to continually reassure one another that you hold that picture as your goal, and in reassuring one another, you create the bond that makes it come true. That is the simplicity and the difficulty of creating a life-long love. It doesn't take much—just everything you've got, and a whole lot of what you're not, yet.

You've been reading this book because you've reached a point in your marriage where you recognize that *something* has to change. Marriage hasn't turned out to be what you expected, but, like every big change in life, marriage opens the door to an entirely different world. Now you have to learn to live in that new world. And you're going to be able to handle it.

A little green sprout

I love to garden. I don't grow anything sensible and useful like lettuce or peas. I just plant flowers, lots of flowers, in every size and color. Two years ago I saw a plant that just knocked me out. It was in a big pot on the front porch of a house, and it was covered in big pink flowers that spilled out over the side of the pot. I took a photograph of the plant to the local plant nursery and they identified the plant as an orchid cactus. I found a grower on the internet who sells these plants. This grower offered so many different kinds, it was hard to choose the ones I wanted. One was more beautiful than the next. I chose as many as I thought I could handle, and within a week I had my cuttings. With these plants, you see, it isn't necessary to buy a growing plant. Just a piece of the plant will take root and grow, if it's handled properly. So instead of a big flowering plant, what I got was a flat piece of a plant, a few inches long and a couple of inches wide.

The directions that came with the cuttings told me what kind of pot to use, and what mixture of ingredients I needed to make up so that the cutting would grow best. The directions also stated that the plants would produce flowers in *two years*! To give me encouragement, the grower had included photographs of each type of flower I had ordered, with the name of the flower printed on the photo.

I carefully planted the flowers as directed, and wrote the name of each type on the side of the pot. Then I waited. After a couple of weeks, several of the cuttings had produced little side branches. And you know what? That was enough. In fact, that was very exciting to see. The dead-looking cuttings that were delivered in a cardboard box had, with the right care, the right feeding, the right amount of light and water, sprung into life. And just that sign of life was enough for me to know I was on my way to a whole lot of flowers!

It's the same way when we start on the road to healing a marriage that seems dead. Just a tiny sprout of life will signify that there is life happening. It doesn't have to be 100% for us to know that we are on the way to something wonderful—and nothing is more wonderful than spending several decades being grateful for a wonderful spouse.

Our nation's Declaration of Independence states that ordinary people have the right to pursue happiness. We are so accustomed to hearing the phrase "the pursuit of happiness," that we often ignore what it means; we take it for granted, when in reality it is a radical idea in human history. I don't know that there has ever been another government that has expressed concern for the happiness of ordinary people. It is a tremendous gift and a tremendous responsibility: we must use this freedom to the utmost, to fulfill our humanity to its highest potential.

What we have before us is the possibility to know real love—love that is tested and proven, love that lasts. It doesn't come served up on a silver platter. But it does come. And it is worth the effort. We are uniquely blessed to live in a time and a place in which we may work toward that end. And there is no better endeavor in which to engage ourselves.

Most of you reading this book have the ability to create the happy marriage that you envisioned for yourselves. If the two of you decide that you will continue until you see good results— that is, if you decide not to quit—you can't miss.

www.ingramcontent.com/pod-product-compliance
Lightning Source LLC
Chambersburg PA
CBHW060443040426
42331CB00044B/2538